To

Jo

Enjoy

Dorothy

To Touch With Love

by

Dorothy Foreman German

authorHOUSE™

1663 LIBERTY DRIVE, SUITE 200
BLOOMINGTON, INDIANA 47403
(800) 839-8640
WWW.AUTHORHOUSE.COM

First published by AuthorHouse 08/02/05

ISBN: 1-4208-6000-3 (sc)
ISBN: 1-4208-6001-1 (dj)

Library of Congress Control Number: 2005904700

Printed in the United States of America
Bloomington, Indiana

This book is printed on acid-free paper.

Dedication

To all who have touched me with love: my parents, George W. Foreman and Naomi Boothe Foreman, family, teachers and friends.

To My Readers:

This book contains thoughts, expectations and experiences I have had along life's way. Through its pages I hope to make your day better and heart a bit lighter as you go with me through Havens of Hope and Highways of Happiness.

> Give not to me praise for these words,
> Though you may wish it so,
> But give Him praise that gave to me
> This talent I may know.
>
> Give not to me a cause of pride,
> Lest I might cease to feel
> That He alone has given me
> These thoughts, these words to seal.
>
> Let's give to Him all praise supreme
> For gifts we each can share –
> He's waiting always just to hear
> Our thanks to Him in Prayer.

>   The Author

Acknowledgements

My indebtedness to Ruth Beymer for her grammatical assistance and gracious manner, both as a friend and critic.

Much credit is due my husband, two daughters and two grandaughters for their enduring patience and constructive criticism. To members of the Indianola Writer's Workshop, thanks for their encouragement and support. And to each of you wonderful Friends whose appreciation and encouragement has prompted my endeavors.

Poems previously published and copyrighted in Iowa Poetry Day Association, Lyrical Iowa, Midstream, and Owings Mills publications.

Iowa Poetry Day Association	1971 – Jet Trail
	Snow Shadows
Lyrical Iowa	1968 – Broken Windmill
Midstream	1973 – Unbeknownst
	1974 – Please Grandma
	Reflection
	1975 – Tomorrow's World
	An Unfilmed Picture
	1976 – Favorite Guests
	Legacy
	Our Daughters
	1977 – After the Rain
	1978 – Pressed Thoughts
	Gulls
	1979 – Wisdom
	1980 – Image Anew
	1981 – Saved From The Auction
	1982 – Across the Street
Rippling Waters / Owings Mills	1996 – Daybreak

Table of Contents

FASCINATIONS

FESTIVITIES

FOLKS

FUN

FAITH

A Little Prayer

A little prayer
       Goes a long, long way.
It brings in sunshine
       On a cloudy day.

A little prayer
       Lifts a burdened load,
And makes travel lighter
       Along life's road.

A little prayer
       Helps an aching heart,
And spurs the weak
       To a strong new start.

A little prayer
       …a thanks to God,
And He'll help you clear
       The path you trod.

Ever mindful
       Of His children's care,
He'll take you through –
       Say a little prayer!

Acceptance

See the wild geese flight design
Like an architect's true line. . .
Blueprints on the sky of time.
    Watch and believe!

Note the opening of the rose. . .
Unfolding buds in sweet repose.
Oh, so much to presuppose.
    Watch and believe!

Heed the task of ant and bee. . .
Without teachers, books or plea,
Busy working endlessly.
    Watch and believe!

Detect the lilacs' fragrant spell,
Tiny violets in the dell,
And the daisies that "won't tell."
    Watch and believe!

Observe the moon and stars so bright,
Evening dusk and black of night,
Break of morn with golden light.
    Watch and believe!

Regard the little sparrow's fall,
The tiny wren's aesthetic call,
Hummingbirds so quick and small.
    Watch and believe!

Discover works of God's great hand,
His mighty ocean and His land;
Even smallest grains of sand.
       Watch and believe!

If you doubt, after all of this,
Pick up God's word and read His bliss.
His promises you cannot miss. . .
       You must believe!

Across the Street

A scarlet crown above a hedge of green
Reminds us of the honor of a Queen.
The red of roses reaching for the sun,
Proclaims above the highest shrub, "I've won!"

Caressed by trim of white in sky-cut roof,
Against a house of gray, you're perfect proof
That someone cares, and therefore gave you birth
By placing you beneath the eaves, in earth.

You must have pushed beyond that lower height
To bring your shining glory to our sight,
And mingled with the morning's diamond dew,
You brighten summer days with jeweled hue.

Reach on---oh climbing rose---feel free to lend
Your beauty to a neighbor and a friend.

Another Carpenter

We watched the tiny Carpenter
As he inched along the house---
Oblivious of our interest
He was quiet as a mouse.

He paused beside our window sill
And built his castle, small and green.
A wax-like structure---golden trim,
The style of which we'd never seen.

For days it poised in warmth of sun
With thread-like anchors holding firm
…this tiny home so full of life
Built by an odd and harmless worm.

And then its door burst open
Exposing now its precious jewel.
The Carpenter had given all
But left another tool.

And there before our eyes unfurled
God's beauty as a priceless dream
…a monarch butterfly emerged
And left an empty shell beside our screen.

A Carpenter---we called him,
Who gave his life that we might see
God's Glory in our own small world
And beauty in a life might be!

Another Carpenter we know
Gave His life for others, too,
That we might beautify the world
Much as the butterfly is meant to do!

Calluses

We've calluses upon our hands

From toiling work or play.

We've calluses upon our feet

From walking every day.

The calluses between our toes

From shoes that do not fit,

All seem to come from constant wear,

From pressure, bumps or hits.

But show to me, I boldly ask,

A man or person rare,

Who has a faintly callused spot

From kneeling down in prayer!

Church Friends

No friends as nice as our friends,

And no friends more true blue,

Few friends do the lovely things

That just ours seem to do.

So we'll remember through the years,

And carry in our heart

A special place for our dear friends

Who make friendship an art!

Country Church

A dear old country church
With a steeple and a bell. . .
Stands firmly in our mem'ries
Holding stories sweet to tell;

That of love and laughter
And a faith it still proclaims,
Standing stately by the wayside
Aged by sunshine, wind and rain.

It was there we met no strangers. . .
God's love we sweetly shared.
No wonder life seemed brighter
There we prayed and loved and cared.

Now, the honeysuckle blossoms
Round the once used old rock well
And the pink wild rose still struggles
Its fragrance to dispel.

The hitchpost, filled each Sunday
Is no longer to be seen. . .
It too, with time has fallen
Among the grasses green.

God's spirit still is present
As it was so long ago,
Like the flowers ever blooming
His message grows and grows.

Daybreak

The opening of God's window
Bursts across the eastern skies - -
Fading night's retreating shadows
As the moonlight slowly dies.

One night the lowly shepherds
Tended flocks with special care
And beheld in awesome wonder
Angels' message in the air.

Then came the glorious morning
Blazing light of Heaven's joys
Bringing peace and love eternal
In God's tiny Baby Boy.

How now can man be doubtful?
As each morning breaks anew
For it brings a Heavenly Blessing
Like the one Christ brings to you.

Everything Is Beautiful

When I was a child with innocent eyes,
My Grandfather taught me to look toward the skies.
We gazed at the rainbow over garden gate
While lonely dove called to a distant mate.

He took me by hand and we slowly strolled through
The Carolina hills still wet with the dew.
Silently he showed me untamed Nature's way - -
From tiny insect to wild life at play.

Butterflies and flowers and blossoming tree
Each one so precious and lovely to see.
The rocks and the rivers and green grassy sod
Grandfather taught me were all works of God.

Lessons he would never allow me to shirk
So he showed me the ants and the bees at work.
The dark rolling rain clouds and bright golden sun
Must each have their way for work to be done.

So mostly while strolling, just Grandpa and me
I learned nature's unfolding splendor, you see.
Everything's beautiful - - when God has His way,
Beauty is waiting for me every day.

Garden of Tomorrow

In your garden of tomorrow,
      Did you plant your flowers today?
Did you sow your seed of kindness
      In a heart that passed your way?

In a corner of that garden,
      Did you drop in friendship's row
A bit of precious sweetness
      To overcome the evil foe?

Did you cast seeds of sympathy
      Beside the bleeding heart?
Or did you leave them on the shelf
      And fail to do your part?

Have you weeded from that garden
      All the burrs of hate and shame?
Have you tended it with patience,
      Tendered not a grudge or blame?

In this plot for future reaping,
      Are you working every day,
Preparing for the harvest
      That is sure to come your way?

Did you surround your plantings
      With a righteous fence of love,
Opened by a gate that's swinging
      By His touch from up above?

If you're reading from His "Guide Book"
    Making plantings by Its guide,
Weeds of evil ne'er shall bother,
    Flowers of joy you'll never hide.

Truly, you must have a garden,
    The Master gave you one to sow.
Love and trust and serve Him daily—
    Life eternal you shall know.

Giving

Give to the world a listening ear
For that is your gift to give,
And mend a broken friendship
With two little words - - "I forgive."

Give a hug to a grieving heart
For that helps a bleeding soul,
So little effort - - but make it a part
Of your caring, loving role.

Give a loving touch to a needed friend.
It can soften the saddest mood.
It is yours to give - - so do it now.
It works like our daily food.

Give a smile to those you meet
For yours, only you can give.
It will bring sunshine along the way
Make life more pleasant to live!

Heavenly Things

We have touched on Heavenly things
  While in this world we trod;
Wild flowers blooming in the spring
  Sown by the hand of God.

The sun that sends its early rays
  Just at the peek of dawn,
Upon a velvet green that grows
  Where there's a well-kept lawn.

The song of birds, their winging flight;
  The sound of breeze that sighs,
And rain that patters through the night
  From lowly clouded skies.

A twinkling star, a full moon's light,
  A rainbow's golden hue;
The murmur of the meadow stream
  With waters clear and blue.

New crops in summer, frost of fall,
  And winter's downy snow;
The ringing of the Church bell's call . . .
  A joyous sound to know.

All these are bits of Heaven
  Before us on Life's screen.
A small preview of more to come
  Than we have ever seen!

Immeasurable

We cannot hold hope
Within our palm,
But certain as some dreams,
We've known its calm!

We cannot hold the wind
        Nor love, within our hand
                And yet, we know that they exist,
                        For by each, we've all been kissed.

Patience, Peace and Kindness,
Laughter and the sound of song --
We cannot reach to touch
And hold -- for long.

We feel the warmth of tenderness
And friendship's joyous treasure,
And lo, we know their wealth,
But not to measure!

Sunlight we cannot grip
        With softest fingertips,
                Although it's there -- this light
                        -- To cradle night.

Thus so with Faith;
We cannot clasp it in our hands
But still we know 'tis there --
The sustenance of man!

Indebted

God gave you a life
To be free from strife
If only you'd follow His way.
He gave you Christ's love,
His gift from above,
If only you'd trust Him each day.

He gave you two eyes
To see beautiful skies,
Two lips to speak oft of Him.
He gave you two hands
To do His commands,
And one heart to keep free of sin.

He gave you two feet,
And courage complete,
To travel the pathway of right.
He gave you His book
In which you can look
To find all you need for a light.

So when Life is past
And you go home at last,
Will you be admitted as one
Who's always been true,
This earthly life through---
Will God say to you, "Well done?"

Indifferent

If we had been in Bethlehem
      two thousand years ago,
Would we have found the Savior
      who had come for us to know?

Would crowds have passed the manger
      with us among them, then---
Unheeding, nor inquiring
      of the One who was within?

Would we have known and passed Him
      just as we do today,
Too busy to be bothered…
      Too rushed to kneel and pray?

Today…we're not in Bethlehem
      and pass no manger dim,
But now we know---and still we fail
      to stop, and worship Him.

Lest We Forget

I shall not forget

     to thank our Lord

For all the wonders

     He has long performed;

And I shall not forget

     there may be shadows,

Of which His Scriptures

     many times have warned.

Then I shall not forget

     to ask His special care for you

Today, tomorrow, and always,

     knowing as we do,

He, too, will not forget!

Little Things

Little drops of water

        make the rivers flow,

Little disappointments

        make our joys grow.

Little rays of sunshine

        make the flowers start,

Little deeds of kindness

        make a happy heart.

Little summer breezes

        make the willows bend,

Little words of courage

        make a lasting friend.

All God's plan and pattern

        make us understand

That "little things" are precious

        and given by His hand!

Little White Church

There's a Little White church
Near an old village square,
Where some friendly folks meet
For a Sunday prayer.

It's a quaint little church
To those who pass by,
With its rose-stained glass
And windows arched high.

Above is a steeple,
A spire, and a bell
That rings every Sunday,
Its worship to tell.

There's a place for you there,
As always you'll know,
When you step through the door
And feel its warm glow.

There's a friendliness sweet---
A handshake---a smile;
The kind that makes living
A joy that's worth while.

And as God watches over
His flock that meets there,
In His Little White Church
Near the old village square,

We know He is happy;
We trust in His care,
As we gather together
In His house of prayer.

My God and I

My God and I have secrets,
He knows my aching heart.
But He can lift the shadows
And give me a new start.

My God and I have secrets,
My fondest dreams He shares.
And though they may be shattered,
I know my God still cares.

My God and I have secrets,
On Him I can depend.
And when all others fail me,
I know that He's my friend.

Our secrets are unnumbered,
We know the reason why.
We walk together daily
…My God and I.

My Master Speaks

Peace be still, the Master once commanded
        and the stormy tempest waves obeyed;
Peace be still, He said unto my heart
        and lo, He made my troubles quickly fade.

Be not afraid, but of good cheer, said Jesus
        to those who watched Him calmly walk the sea
And now I find myself today rejoicing
        Be not afraid, He too, has said to me.

Be opened, He said to the deaf one---
        to me He also said the same,
For He gave me desire for seeking
        the truths within His Book of Fame!

Deny thyself, He once requested---
        take up the cross and follow me,
And then He spoke unto the blind man,
        go thy way, thy faith has made thee see.

Take heed and watch, He warned them,
        for ye know not the hour I come.
Now, I too, the cross must carry
        and watch until Life's battle's won.

Go ye and teach my gospel
        to all the world, He also said,
These I found in Mark's great writings---
        You, too, have found them if you've read.

New Things

Since you have gone I'll live alone,

I'll find new things to do;

I'll go new places, see new sights,

And make new dreams come true.

I too, shall learn to think new thoughts

And learn to sing new songs;

I'll cast my troubles to the winds

And somehow get along.

I'll build new castles somewhere else,

I'll find new paths to trod,

But there will be a steadfast strength---

The friend I have in God.

Peace

It's not the stilling of the gun

or victory cries when battle's won;

It's not the end of long protests

of marching men---ungainly quests;

It's not when law has forced command

and calmed the riots of the land.

"The fruit of the spirit" brings release,

"To the fruit of Righteousness comes Peace."

---Peace must come to the heart within,

from God to loving, praying men.

Sewing for the Master

You are the Master's seamstress.
Choose your pattern with great care;
For it, you know, is the secret
Of your finished garment fair.

The one and only pattern
Is the one of Christ, dear friend.
With God's book of full instructions,
Your best work will safely end.

Now cut with shears of kindness
Around all these pieces true,
Leaving out the ease of hatred –
Tracing darts of joy through.

Pins of great humility
And those of devotion, too,
Will keep this pattern well attached
To the best material – you.

Next, place right sides together
Pinning yours with God's supreme,
Now you're ready for the stitching
On your Precious Life's Machine.

Use silver threads of worship
Where there is greatest strain,
Reinforcing this weak garment
With the best you can obtain.

Use golden thread for stitching---
That of love so sweet and pure...
A bobbin full of faith and hope
To make your seams secure.

Hem it, protected always
With a fervent, earnest prayer;
And press it now with love again
To remove the pleats of care.

Wear this finished garment
Every long and single day...
You are the Master's seamstress---
Show it now, and all the way.

Spaceship Christianity

There's a Spaceship just for travel
O'er a route we each must take.
Its capacity is boundless---
It's the one kind of its make.

It is powered by a rocket
Instilled in Christian hearts;
Excels in all its tryouts,
for the Bible is its chart.

The Pilot's never weary.
He's always there on call
To keep it in its orbit
And be sure it does not fall.

Like the leaders of our country
He, too, likes volunteers
To make its flight successful
And to calm all human fears.

This ship requires attention;
So at once, my friends, prepare
To refuel it every Sunday
And daily with a prayer!

Be not the one to falter
On this mission flight, supreme;
For this Spaceship's built for travel.
It is not a man-made dream!

Take Heart

When days may seem to turn to night,

And darkness overshadows light;

When trials are more than we can bear,

And every hour is filled with care...

    Take heart---for God is near.

When sunshine turns to clouds of gray,

And hope seems crushed with each new day;

When life is curtained with despair

And trouble seems to us unfair...

    Take heart---for God is near.

And if our prayers seem all unheard,

Our joys dispelled, our vision blurred;

There's love beyond our human touch

For each of us---a priceless crutch.

    Take heart---for God is near.

The Edge of Tomorrow

Today is the edge of tomorrow –

    Make it the best that you can,

It never returns for a moment,

    For life presses on in its span.

The future is weighed by the present,

    Shadowed quite oft by the past,

Today we can help tomorrow

    If we make its presence last.

Live on this edge of tomorrow

    So when it quickly moves on,

Your worth will be remembered

    After today is gone.

Unforeseen

Just when days were the brightest

    And dreams began to come true;

A home and loved ones to cherish---

    And skies seemed ever so blue!

Just when days were so perfect,

    Complete from sunrise to sunset---

Working and toiling so simply,

    With never a thought of regret.

Just when days seemed the sweetest

    At the age that trials seem few---

A cloud rolled in o'er the sunshine

    And severed Life's Golden Hue!

So now, when days again brighten

    Ever with memory's ties;

Dear God, we mean not to falter,

    But we always will wonder, just why?

November 25, 1944

Vacation Majesty

We saw God on vacation
    As the way unraveled miles.
We saw Him in men's faces,
    In weary travelers' smiles.

We saw Him at the table
    Where young hearts bowed their heads,
Where reverently and quietly
    Their grateful thanks were said.

We saw Him in the grassland
    Where nimble antelope play.
He was there in early morning
    And at the close of day.

We saw Him where the waters
    Of the mighty rivers flow;
We saw Him in the mountains
    Where their tops were white with snow.

We saw Him in the mudpots
    And the geysers' steam so high;
We saw Him in "Old Faithful"
    As it spouted towards the sky.

We saw His splendor glowing
    In the mist above the falls;
Where the colors of the rainbow
    Arched across the canyon walls.

Yes, we saw Him in the canyons
    That no other hand could mold;
In the wonders of the Tetons
    And the pines so tall and old.

We saw Him in His beauty
    Where the mountain flowers grew,
In the graceful moving wildlife
    As they came and left our view.

We saw Him, yes, we met Him
    In a million drivers' seats,
Where only His commanding
    Could have made our trip complete.

We were in His presence daily,
    Always conscious of Him there.
Yes, we saw God on vacation...
    We saw Him everywhere.

Vespers

In evening's hush we walked in twos,
　　Along a narrow way,
Quietly down a rugged path
　　We humbly went to pray.

Inspiring silence touched our hearts.
　　At the trail's end there shone
Afloat the Lakeshore water
　　A fire in glimmering tones.

Its light reflected on a cross
　　Upon a quiet lake,
And we remembered Him who gave
　　A life for our own sake.

Together then we entered
　　This open chapel there,
And sat in solemn reverence
　　For long and silent prayer.

Before us lay the waters,
　　So lifeless, calm and still.
It seemed as if Christ walked them
　　And they obeyed His will.

Above, the heavens blessed us
　　With summer's moonlit sky,
Interspersed with downy clouds,
　　So lazy there on high.

Around us lay the wildwood,
    The art of God's own hand,
Reminding us that He had made
    This grand and glorious land.

The fire by the cross flickered;
    And as it ebbed away,
Old hymns echoed our praises
    Ending a perfect day.

Voices

The wind has many voices---
A gentle, soothing breeze,
A kiss that softly touches,
Yet oft time likes to tease.

Fresh laundry flips in sunshine
To dry by rays of gold,
Assisted by a version
Of wind, that too, can scold.

Sometimes we hear the anger
When it rages day or night,
With strength beyond man's power
To stop its ugly flight.

A rustle in the Cedars
When winter ice appears
---a crisp and crackling rattle
Tells us Wind is speaking near.

When dark clouds roll with thunder
And trees are forced to sway,
We know the turbulent Heavens
Have company today.

So gentle, kind and needed---
Yet strong and rough it blows
And many sounds it creates
With sun and rain and snow.

God too, has many voices
"Be still, My child." He sighs,
"Know Me, hear Me…Listen---
I will hear your every cry."

Worldly Values

A famous man once proudly claimed---
"I've wealth beyond a measure.
I've more than any millionaire
Can count within his treasure."

"I'll never want for anything,
With what I've put away.
For I've a million memories
To keep me every day."

And though this gentleman was blessed
With much in worldly gold---
His heart was filled with other wealth
And happiness untold.

For memories are a priceless gift
We're given each to keep.
No man can take them from us
For his own fame to reap.

No man can count his unweighed wealth
Except the one who owns,
And most of them are reaped from seed
That he and God have sown.

Worship Time

Sunday morning in Heaven

    Must be such a joyous time.

When all of God's children singing

    Is heard in melodious chime.

How softly the old hymns echo

    Floating out from the churches clear,

To the Golden Throne of Glory

    For God and His angels to hear!

Yes, Sunday morning in Heaven

    Must be a sweet time, too,

When Church prayers said in unison,

    Ascend through celestial blue.

Then after the prayers and praises

    There must be a silence divine,

When God looks down and blesses

    His children with fullness sublime.

FASCINATIONS

After the Rain

The sun played peek-a-boo today
As a child darts through a crowd.
Behind the skies huge aprons
Of soft and creamy clouds.

Peek-a-boo to a drenched lush earth
With rain-pierced veins engraved
On rolling sweep of clean fresh soil
Where Spring's young grain had waved.

Peek-a-boo to the world below
And the earth played with the sun,
Between those clouds of touch-me-nots
….The game was childish fun.

For seldom had the Daystar shone
Enhancing sphere of late;
Old Jupiter had been busy
Pouring out his cup of fate.

April Showers

The tearful clouds move swiftly
    Above dry and thirsty earth,
        And cry their crystal julep
            For Springtime's blessed birth.

The fields drink slow and surely,
    Nursing plants and trees and seed
        With the pure and cooling nectar
            Supplying strength they need.

The tiny sprouts push upward,
    And the blades of grain appear
        While swollen buds burst open---
            No mistaking time of year!

April? Ah, yes April!
    Your clouds have slipped away,
        And left you royal treasure
            To hand to waiting May.

Beautiful Iowa

There's a place in mid-America
Where the earth is vitalized,
It's known as the state of Iowa,
Her wealth is not disguised.

You can HEAR her growing majesty
In the song of big machines,
Or the voice of her people singing
As they fulfill their dreams.

You can SEE her warmth and kindness
As you travel from east to west;
From north or south to her borders
It's her folks you like the best.

You can GROW with her youth in knowledge
In a college or in a school;
Feel peace under sacred steeples,
And be shown the Golden Rule.

You can SAIL her many waters
Or float with balloons on high,
Hike in her parks, or camp there,
The choice is yours to try.

You can FEEL her love unbounding
Wherever you walk, it is there,
In country, town or city
Iowa just seems to care.

You can DRIVE for miles unending
On ribbons of super slab,
Through great tall corn and meadows—
A pattern like woven plaid.

Beautiful Iowa, we love you,
May your spirit always be
The greatest of all in the nation,
Sheltering your wealth so free.

Broken Windmill

Almost majestic, now it stands,

An emblem of a passing age,

Rebuked by only wind and rain

Which gnarls the oak to rugged stage.

Almost protective, too, it seems---

Towering on high,

Amid a farmyard calm and still,

Flanked by an autumn sky.

Almost forgotten---

This windmill's needed past,

Yet like our young of yesteryears

Its work is done at last.

Time presses on---

To youth old age gives way,

And so the broken windmill stands

Symbolic of another day.

Chapters of Life

In life's Book, from dawning to sunset,
Each chapter is precious to know,
But few of us realize its presence
As down through the ages we go.

Is it that time when we're infants
Cuddled close in our mother's arms?
Or is it when childhood adventure
Holds us tight in magnetic charm?

Can it be when youth tugs our heartstrings---
Reluctant to all else but fun?
Or might it be only when romance
Has settled our hearts upon one?

Perhaps it's the time as young parents
We fondly observe childish play;
Or is it when middle age finds us
Content with the things of the day?

Would you say that nearer the sunset
Joys sweeter to us seem to be,
As we dwell in much reminiscing
O'er a past we now fully see?

No doubt you might choose from these phases
A time doubly sweet, that is true,
But always there's happiness present.
Its absence depends upon you.

As long as there's a deep understanding,
And wherever there's love to be found,
Your book will have happy chapters
Each page with joy will abound.

As author of your life's story
Only you can fill it with zest,
Today, tomorrow and always,
Write it well---each day can be best.

Childish Delight

There are some things that never escape the memory. Many grow dim with the turn of the years, and often one cannot recall a once familiar name, the time a certain incident took place or perhaps even the spot. But in childish ideals there are some things that remain forever.

The smell of fresh baked bread, the touch of a soft, flimsy flower picked in the wildwood; the glow of an open fire where creamy marshmallows became fat brown hats on a stick; the purr of the first kitten we can remember calling our own; and that weird lonely echo of the old hoot owl that made us pull the sheets tight around our tousled heads and be glad we were tucked safely in bed.

Childhood brings back the thought of the first frogs in the spring, croaking with all their might to out do the dozens of others in competition; the first new lambs---wobbly at first but soon playful and full of energy; downy baby chicks and yellow ducks; green little goslings that stretched their necks to talk to anyone or thing that happened to pass while they grabbed bits of grass between gabs and covered amazing distances as they did so. Jenny Wren always had a sassy word or two and there were robins that returned year after year for their home in the evergreens.

But these take second place on my list of memories.

In a little village only a short walk from the place I fondly called home, lived a dear old lady known to all as "Aunt Mag." Aunt Mag was actually an aunt of my father's and had taken him under her wing when he was a young man and his own parents moved to another state to homestead. It was while he lived here that he married the grandest girl in the world – my mother, so I will never know how much I really owed Aunt Mag. At the time I recall, I was a small child, perhaps five years old, but the things I remember about her are numerous. Though she spoke quickly to children and often times frightened us, we were certain that somewhere hidden in an apron pocket or a teacup were bits of peppermint candy or cookies she would share with us before we left her presence.

Aunt Mag was a large lady and she suffered intensely with rheumatism and spells of asthma. In fact, her breathing at times was enough to scare any child and yet we loved her. She lived in a small cottage edged with flowers---roses, flowering almonds, lilacs and gorgeous white snowballs. I can almost see now the huge bleeding heart that stood beside the always-welcome door. She loved company and everyone was invited in.

She wore small gold-rimmed spectacles and her gray hair was pulled back from a round plump face and wound in a small knot at the back of her head. She wore a waist apron almost always over brown calicos. I remember her Bible was ever within reach and It she read daily.

But the outstanding bit that stayed with me through the years was the hat shop she operated in her own home. Oh no, she had no fancy hat stands, no counters or models, and in a three roomed house there was little extra space in the beginning. But boxes came by the numbers and there was a place found for each of them. Some times they were put away under the bed or stacked high in any room of the house and brought out only when a customer desired another style or color.

The fragrance that erupted---and to a small child it seemingly did erupt---from those boxes when they were opened is beyond any description I have ever read or ever could hope to imagine! The smell of sweet, fresh straw mingled with that of shellac and the newness of those hats brought out from layers of crinkled white tissue was almost more than a childish nose or eyes could stand. There was fragrance and beauty combined. Ribbons, beads, net, bits of artificial fruit and large colorful plumes decorated those perfumed items.

I remember few hats that my mother bought, but I remember dozens that she looked at and it was sheer delight to hear that a new shipment of millinery had arrived at Aunt Mag's for we had only to stop by for a minute and we simply had to see the latest and always there was that exotic odor to accompany the beauty---a freshness never to be forgotten---the most fragrant memory of my childhood.

Country Village

There's a place in old North Missouri
Where a village once prospered and grew,
It was small, yet within it was centered
A feeling that folks wanted you.

The town itself now has vanished.
Only those who remember can know
The spot where Pawnee once flourished
And folks miles around learned to go.

The hitchpost is gone with the ruins
Of buildings once sturdy and strong;
And cars swiftly pass on the roadway
Where buggies once traveled along.

The rain comes and goes with the sunshine
As it did in the days of yore
When the folks sat around on nail kegs
Chatting in the old Country Store.

The crossroads remain as an emblem
Small flowers bloom year after year,
Though wild grasses smother their beauty;
Their fragrance is ever as dear.

Roses twine where the gateways
Once welcomed the laughter of friends.
And the snowballs' pure white clusters
Cause stately branches to bend.

The peonies, nestled in silence
'Neath the evergreen's tender bough,
Send forth their rare pink picture,
Defying the years passing now.

Even the fruit trees' splendor
Of blossoms and gifts they bear,
Live on as a special memory,
For those who once gave them care.

And still on a bright spring morning,
Drifting out over sweet country air,
Comes the call of the birds, as of always,
When the village people dwelled there.

To some these are fond reminders
As they stop for a glance of the past;
To others it's only a hilltop,
Its meaning is fading at last.

But to those who lived and loved it,
There's nothing can ever erase
The memories pleasantly cherished
Of this precious old Pawnee place.

Gulls

Afloat on rhythmic wings of white---
Silent, in another realm
They seek their way 'mid misty heights
And they alone are at the helm.

"Oh, ship ahoy," below, they trace you
Follow as you steam away,
Graceful on the wind's soft kisses
Sailing out beyond the bay.

On out to sea they soon will leave you,
They, too, have voyages to make,
Not only you "Oh ship of Mercy"---
Gulls have journeys they must take!

Heritage Vision

A dormant memory lives.
Yet, amid our rush, memories are buried;
Swallowed by the hustle of modern living;
Uncovered only by those who stop to remember,
Stop to be mindful.

Memory is a gift unequaled,
Past events revived.
Memories of transportation...carriages huge and black,
Drawn by shiny, high-stepping horses, across bumpy roads
                                                    or streets;

Buggies which took us surely over muddy country lanes;
Ponies...lively, graceful ponies! Thrilling to ride!
Stages...business needed these to thrive.
And sleighs...gliding sleighs that skimmed through
                                    dreamlands of snow and ice!

Memory holds these.
Today they are replaced,
Superceded by swifter moving vehicles
Making use of but one element---Time.
Faster! Faster!

Time in memory moved slowly.
There was time to laugh and love and live.
Now time is consumed---spent.
Oh memory, grant us a desire to love you and brace us
                                for this time in which we live;
To love and laugh and be thankful in the future for a
                                memory of this present day.

Image Anew

The old woodbine caught the glory
    Of the late September sun
Beaming through the sturdy walnut
    Just before the day was done.

Autumn splashes with the colors
    Of its deep and rustic red
Melted into evening splendor
    Brushed by breezes overhead.

The real glory of this setting
    Was not caught by camera eye,
But by mirror, shone resplendent,
    Like a picture one might buy.

Brighter than an artist's brushes
    Ever copied such a scene,
It depicted the old walnut
    Dressed as stately as a queen.

I know not for whom this mirror
    Had reflected sights before,
But I know God had a hand in
    Working through that open door.

For I glimpsed His chosen Handwork
    In a new and different way---
This old walnut dressed in woodbine
    And the golden sun's late ray.

I had watched this same transition
    Over years as fall appeared,
But that shining oval mirror
    Made the picture more endeared.

Jet Trail

Across the crystal blue above

Before horizons meet,

There spreads a "Daylight Milky Way,"

Man's accomplished feat!

Though only seconds have elapsed,

Since plane slipped swiftly by---

A U.S. jet has left its trail---

White path across the sky!

A path that marks another age;

This era, yours and mine;

Oh Future, you must hold much more---

For progress moves with time.

Keepsakes

Today I found some souvenirs
Tucked lovingly away,
And mem'ries flooded o'er my mind
With thoughts of yesterday.

For first I found some baby shoes
Once worn by tiny feet,
And then a little velvet dress,
Tattered---crushed, but sweet.

Two locks of hair---each tied with blue,
One long and curly brown,
The other, short and auburn red
Pinned to a yellowed gown.

I found with these a picture book
Of songs and nursery rhymes,
Two broken dolls, a small tea set
With cups the size of dimes.

A workbook each for spelling,
Reading and language, too,
Some 4-H ribbons in a box…
Some white, red ones and blue.

And then some high school letters,
Some snapshots and some notes,
A pressed corsage, a banquet book
Scrolled with humorous quotes.

How years flew by in misty thoughts
As I handled these with care.
Each held a perfect dream for me
Complete beyond compare.

Memories

How
    like
        the
           stars---
               our
                  memories,
A
    constant
        and
           eternal
              bliss!
They
    both
        are
          lights
             of
                God,
And
    each
        a
          gift
            of
              His.
So
   in
      your
        mem'ry
           may
             you
               hold

The
      lasting
            friendships
                        you
                              have
                                    known. . . .
Reflections
            of
                  a
                        light
From
      love
            that
                  you
                        have
                              sown!

Night Storm

The black of evening hours
Stole in with the hidden moon,
And slithered across the valley
With a soft wind's gentle tune.

Something about the darkness
Whispered God's lullaby,
To dying days' departure
And the mourner's muffled cry.

This night edged in…reliving
The work and restless play
That come with Sunlight windows
Which open and close the day.

A hush came with the darkening
And settled in with the night;
---Awesome, but quickly swallowed
By a storm cloud's ugly sight.

Then the tumbling thunder
And the splintered lightening crack
Moved in to break the silence…
Trimming sky with bright ric rac.

The mystery of the nightfall
With its magic molded form
Became a raging image
With the forces of the storm.

Sometimes we scarcely notice
How God's Miracles repeat
The message of His Power---
His strength, with no defeat.

But stormy nights remind us
That He still is in command,
For no earthly means have conquered
A Night Storm o'er the land!

O'er Window Sill

I gaze from o'er my window sill
Across the green of yonder hill,
And ask as now I dwell in peace
"Will God's great wonders ever cease?"

For only yesterday it seems
I had a different window scene.
It too, I cherish in my heart
A memory that will ne'er depart.
From clouds which lowered from aloft,
There came a blanket...downy soft,
And dressed yon hill in snowy white---
A veiling of a glorious sight!
Peaks and winding little swirls
Glistened in the light like pearls,
And though 'twas shrouded too, in cold
That picture in my mind I hold.

Today, I find the blanket green,
Edged by a silver ribboned stream,
And Cattle graze before my eyes,
As if in greatest paradise!

This Prairie sight...it's great to see,
Especially for someone like me.
For this great magic I adore...
Tomorrow, there shall still be more!
A carpet browned by burning sun
Will cover hill when Summer's done,
Then though to some its beauty leaves---
Not so to me...I do not grieve.
For well I know Life dwells there yet,
And this I never shall forget,
There's scenery always from yon hill
As I look o'er my window sill!!

Pressed Thoughts

Creases in my countenance,

Furrows on my brow,

Are visible to others

And always show somehow.

But the wrinkles in my heart

Are those you never see,

Memories of a lifetime

Meant for only me!

Purple Violets

Fragile beauty in a royal gown,

    A woodland queen with a priceless crown!

Thirstily drinking the evening dew,

    Basking in warmth of the sunshine, too.

If you could speak it would be in song

    Touching the hearts of the busy throng;

But ah, your beauty is enough for me,

    Silent little violet of rich luxury!

Roses

God gave me a garden

          to love and to tend

He gave me its rosebuds

          to share with a friend

They bring their sweet fragrance

          and bright vivid hue

With all my good wishes

          And much love to you!

Saved From the Auction

She arrived late. Perhaps the relative who brought her had purposely waited. There was little time to look over her possessions.

She came from the nursing home with a small black suitcase to attend the household auction. An Auction prepared by others—not sanctioned by her but allowed, since she could physically no longer live alone.

She walked unattended into the empty house, wandering through each familiar room. It would never be home again.

Outside once more, low clouds dipped, trying to fade out attached memories. Occasionally the sun helped to sustain them.

The auctioneer chanted. Laughter and bids mingled. She scarcely heard. She was looking for some keepsakes and said she would like to buy a few. A concerned bystander informed her they were still hers and would cost her nothing.

She picked up some small items---unfinished crocheted articles, some embroidery work---perhaps others unseen or unnoticed and tucked them into the little bag.

The last thing I saw in her toil-worn wrinkled hands was a pair of baby shoes, also wrinkled and worn. I thought of my own infant's booties at home in the bureau drawer. Would this one day happen to me? My heart cried, "No," but then reality flashed, and I knew it might.

Snow Shadows

Shadows on new fallen snow,
Like Jack Frost's splendid art,
Depict distorted figures
As hate does in the heart.

Objects change dimensions
With winter's soft moonlight,
And seemingly misguided,
Grow tall upon the white.

Cities, farms and country,
Interspersed with trees,
Cast silent calm reflections
Patterned with great ease.

Shadows on new fallen snow,
Etched softly, dark and still,
Are pictures on a canvas
Untouched by pen or quill.

Spirit Lake

I heard the rhythmic melody
Of the waves upon the sand…
A perfected drum of music,
Beating on the old lake's strand.

I slept in peaceful slumber
From a lullaby so soft,
Though man-made noises echoed
On the ground, and from aloft.

I woke to notes repeating
The sweet music of the night,
Refreshed by sounds so restful
And the air so pure and light.

The migrating Monarchs' presence
Added to this joyous dawn,
As they left their night-time clusters
Floating o'er dew-draped lawn.

As the sunlight kissed the morning
With its warm and golden hue,
Spirit Lake became a mirror
Reflecting clear glass, smooth and blue.

And I fancied in my memory
How in those days of yore
The Indians saw these same old haunts
Camping near old Spirit's shore.

How the Redmen, too, had marveled
As the days began anew
And they found these passive waters
Waiting for their light canoes.

Waters as I too, now found them;
Morning shadows on the sand…
Moments to remember, always
Of this nation's Nature Land.

Spirit of America

The American Spirit...from whence does it come?
Out of the blue and under the sun;
Over the hilltops, mountains and streams---
There comes the challenge---the American dream.

A dream of the future, a flame that is fanned
By waving Old Glory throughout the land.
By thoughts and by vision of the Lady so great
Who welcomes the World at Freedom's gate.

The Lady...ah beauty with her special crown!
Standing so tall for this Nation renown!
She's the Symbol of Justice, of great History,
Represents Independence and sweet Liberty.

She, too, flanks our Spirit with majesty bold
Her Crown and her Torch must shine as of old.
We'll keep Her, rebuild Her and always She'll be
A part of this Country for people to see.

The Flag and the Lady we hold with esteem,
A part of the past and all future dreams,
In the hearts of Her People this Spirit survives,
It's an indwelling part of American Lives.

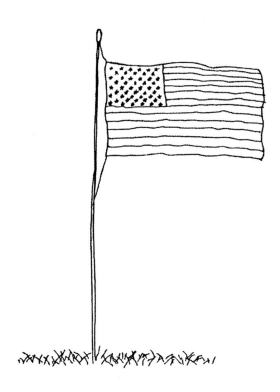

Summer's Change

Down the dusty lane
Apple blossoms swing
High on barren boughs,
And they defy the unseen strength
Which forces them to sway;
For it is not yet time for them to float away
On shifting winds.
They have still to be kissed by busy bees
Or lovely butterflies...
Still to raise their silent beauty to the skies.

So delicately pink---these blossoms
Casting fragrant spells
On those who pass;
So dainty, these---such magic
That they shall turn to be
Red, red apples on a tree!

The Millennium Mouse

The Millennium Mouse surely got loose,

Or else got in to high powered juice---

For he messed up our political plan

And now we don't know who is our man.

Patience…good people

There'll be one who will win,

And some day we'll find out

The man that got in !!!

The Return

I went back one day to a homestead
Nestled down among rolling hills,
My heart skipped a beat as I marveled
At the change from Time's rugged skills.

At first the beauty seemed vanished,
…A longing for which I'd returned.
I felt sick at heart o'er my coming
And things I had hoped for, and yearned.

I couldn't help listening for footsteps
Or a voice to call out my name.
With thoughts flashing back to the present
I pondered the reason I came.

I found, as I lingered a moment,
The strangeness departed with ease---
It was home; and though years had marred it,
My love for it never would cease.

I found no one there to greet me,
Not even old Spud, our prized dog.
Tears came and clouded my vision;
I was a lone ship in a fog!

The cottage no longer was spotless
Rusty screens and doors were ajar.
The wind whistled through broken windows,
The old windmill creaked from afar.

As aged walls circled about me,
Now empty deserted and cold
I visioned each room so distinctly,
As it was in the days of old.

I turned to a small vacant bedroom,
The place of my own infant birth.
I thought of its warmth as a youngster
Through illness and Hide-and-Seek mirth.

A little mouse scampered before me,
Away from the old chimney shelf;
While I again challenged my memory...
Alone, in the past by myself.

I closed out the world, but heard music
That once brought such great joy to me:
My mother's piano was ringing---
Crazy mind---what a fantasy!

For even old Frank, our pet pigeon,
I thought I could hear and see,
Remembering his pacing antics
Across those same black and white keys.

The lessons taught then and remembered
So vividly swept back to mind:
Sweet love, tender hearts and compassion
Are riches sometimes hard to find.

I found these the things that were timeless
Clustered down in depths of my heart.
Despite other fond recollections
I knew it was time to depart.

I left the old house to the ages,
To the mystic change of the years.
Nostalgia had rendered a purpose,
Now content, I left with my tears.

The Seasons

Winter Expects...

      Pictures from <u>October</u>'s album
          <u>November</u>'s song of harvest intake;
      Resounding joy...<u>December</u>'s fun,
          Blanket warmth of Christmas snow flakes.

      Frigid pains of <u>January</u>
          Relieved by streams of melting snow,
      When Spring's bleak <u>February</u>
          Bows to Summer's meek hello!

Summer Ponders...

      Kisses from <u>March</u> lullabies,
          Bathing in sweet <u>April</u> showers,
      A rainbow halo o'er dark skies
          And a dress of <u>May</u>---bright flowers.

      The rose perfume of early <u>June</u>,
          A healing warmth of <u>July</u> sun.
      Romantic arms of <u>August</u> moon
          And sweet sleep when <u>September</u>'s done.

Tomorrow's World

I saw tomorrow today

In the faces of a thousand young people.

I saw them laugh, and knew tomorrow would be happy;

I saw them calm after a storm, and I knew tomorrow could
    have peace.

I saw them with books and knew their future held wisdom;

I saw them disagree and knew tomorrow would have problems.

But I saw them share with one another and I knew tomorrow would
    have love!

Unbeknownst

This town,
     Your town,
          Our town.

Asleep with night's shear curtains drawn!
Within its varied homes the people rest,
Not mindful of the beauty they have closed their eyes upon.
The softened shadows -- an Artist's perfect work;
Moonbeams and stars that never cease their wonders great to share!
The rustle of the night's own breeze -- a soothing cooling air,
Remote from days.

Once too, another town slept, peaceful.
Oh, Bethlehem of old,
Where people sought to rest from busy day!
There, too, were dreams and night's sweet recompense.
Calm and quiet night for those so spent,
Unknowing that before the break of morn
The world would bow on bended knee beside a baby born
In stable low,
They did not know.

And so, this town sleeps on,
Unthinking of the morrow's fame it too may shelter.
Yet it shall wake to such abundant wealth!
Flowers sprinkled with night's tears;
Day's touch of gentleness,
Sweet scented air,
The gay and joyful squeals of children
Aglow with happy thoughts of self.
The greeting of a neighbor.
Amid the busy day it will not be aware,
Nor will it care --

Of riches great, and glowing health,
Nor will it take the time to know its wealth.
Ordinary things and ordinary folks
Like us in
      This town,
           Your town,
                Our town.

Where Is Love?

Why do families stray apart?
Making strangers of their hearts?
Where are the hugs once loved so much?
What happened to our family touch?
        Where did love go?

Too busy for a cheery call?
And letters we don't write at all.
A little visit now and then –
When was the last? Remember when?
        Where did love go?

Dear Ones we need togetherness
A bit more joy and happiness
We need our family strength to share
To know and feel each other's care –
        Where did love go?

I often wonder if there still is time
To repair this love of yours and mine.
But if we start this very day
The Lord will surely show the way –
        Where did love go?

Wildwood Echoes

Wild flowers scent the timberland,
White clouds ride the sky.
The ripples at the old creek's bend,
Harmonize with the wren's soft cry.

Turtle doves in the distance call;
Screeching hawks sail o'er
While I today wild berries seek,
I think of old pals more and more.

Cottontails rustle through the grass,
A squirrel scampers by,
Butterflies flutter here and there
And noisy bees beside me fly.

'Mid all these things there seems to be
Echoes far away.
'Tis childish voices calling me
Back to a childhood happy day.

When once we scorned the worldly cares
Tramping wooded land,
And laughingly we picked the briars
From scratched and youthful sunbrowned hands.

These selfsame haunts I roam alone---
Now they make me sad.
But I am glad they're in my heart
Sweet recompense for things once had.

Winter Observation

Little snowbird on the wing,
You're such a cute and winsome thing;
Lively hops on heaped up snow,
How far will you really go?

Oh little puffball; with a spring
Inside those threads of leg and wing,
You must chill when North winds blow
Mid shrubs and branches hanging low.

Little finch of gray and white,
Weather doesn't help your plight,
Yet vim and vigor you display
In such a sweet and humble way.

Baby bunting, dressed so right,
Feathered with a cape for flight,
Quick to sense approaching harm,
Flying off with such alarm!

Where do you go, wee chickadee
When nights so cold are bad for me?
You're always back when comes the morn.
Where did you sleep, and were you warm?

'Tis plain to me that I must see
God watches you as he does me.
His care for you in winter time
Proves He will care for me and mine!

Wisdom

It takes so long for us to learn

The lesson all should know...

That love can really change the world,

If love is seed we sow!

Your Invoice

It no doubt is good to have money
  And lots of the things it can buy,
But make a list for your records,
  Of the things that don't come so high.

Have you ever purchased a friendship?
  Or a neighbor's admiring glance?
His smile, his handclasp, his kindness,
  When it seems you've had your last chance?

Have you ever priced a character…
  The kind we would all like to be?
It just can't be bought in silver,
  It takes years to build, but it's free.

There's no price to pay for the sunsets,
  The songs of the birds in the trees;
Patter of rain on the rooftops,
  Or the gentle touch of the breeze.

The scent of the wildflower blossoms,
  The fragrance of sweet new mown hay;
The call of the owl in darkness,
  Or the sight of the break of day.

The faith, hope and dreams of the future,
  Clinging love of a pure young heart;
Baby's kiss, or his soft footsteps,
  …No price, but each rich in its art.

So count not your wealth by your money,
  You are rich and may not know why,
For the things that we take for granted
  Neither silver nor gold can buy.

FESTIVITIES

A Long-Ago Spook Night

A big old orange moon that night
Peeped over a Midwest hill,
When two young teenage Spooks set forth
For a Halloween big thrill!

They bounced along---her hand in his
As they thought of pranks to play,
"Let's go to old man Smith's," said she
…He agreed without delay.

So on they tripped, still hand in hand
'Til they found the dark dim street;
No light around and not a sound
When they knocked to get their treat.

By now their fun had just begun
'Twas time for a trick or two,
So they looked around to quickly find
A special prank to do.

They headed toward the old back house
Down the path that led the way---
This old time trick would be such fun
And really make their day!

They crouched along the autumn stems
Of the frosted Hollyhocks
And made a dash for cover
Behind some tall lilacs.

They giggled as they sneaked along
But before they reached their goal
Old Mister Smith's dog, Rover
Pounced from the clothesline pole.

His chain was barely long enough
To reach these kids at play
But he caught Todd's baggy britches
And tore the seat away!

By this time Ruth had vanished
As swift as frightened deer
And back to mom's she headed,
Leaving Todd with all his fear.

He never caught her on that run
As she covered "no man's land"
She left him far behind right then
…No time to hold his hand.

Now Todd had such explaining
To his Mom who patched his pants
But Halloween was his excuse
When night spooks take their chance.

Old Mister Smith's still laughing
For he watched this funny scene
From dark windows in his kitchen
On that spooky Halloween!

The old Outhouse and Rover
Makes a story fun to tell
And many a spook remembers
Such Halloweens as well.

Now Todd and Ruth are speaking
And have long since come to say,
"Halloween is great fun time---
When Spooks go out to play!

Back Home at Christmas

We'll be making snowballs
And sliding down hill
      Under the stars that shine.
For we'll all be together
At home this year,
      Back home at Christmas time.

The old house has waited
For ten long years
      This returning mirth to entwine,
So we'll gather inside
'Round the Christmas tree
      Back home at Christmas time.

As always Luke's story
We will softly read
      And miss not a single line.
We'll love every moment
And treasure them all,
      Back home at Christmas time!

Belated
Happy Birthday

We may not think as quickly
And move a whole lot less,
'Cause birthdays change so many things
We surely must confess.

But somehow I remember
Friends along the way,
Who touched my life and made me smile;
And so to you I say---

"Hope you had a happy birthday
On October's late fall day,
For birthdays are a choice of God,
He wills them His own way!!

Christmas Greeting

Our Christmas card came early
On a late November day.
The postman didn't bring it,
Nor train, nor bus, nor pay.

It came without a postage stamp
And U.P. played no part
In making the delivery
To our home and to our heart.

For glancing through our window
From a warm and cozy place
We saw a beauteous wonder –
A white coverlet of lace.

There seemed to be a message
To remind us of the time,
And what a joy it gave us
As we gazed at every line!

A snow storm had descended
On our city through the night
And brought to us reminders,
With a grand and glorious sight.

A laden pine, a snow capped roof,
A lamp post dressed in white,
A picket fence with fluffy hats,
Were pictures of delight.

So each of us need only look
From window to our yard,
To see this special Season's note –
Our Master's Christmas Card!

Christmas Living

Each year we make our Christmas list,
With gifts for one and all;
From baby's precious rattle,
To dear Grandma's woolen shawl.

We don't forget the mailing
Of Christmas cards with cheer,
To all our friends so distant
Who expect them once a year.

We work and save our pennies,
Buying Christmas trees and lights---
Decorations for our windows,
For the Season's days and nights.

Oh yes, it's quite commercial,
These Christmas things we do;
But for every single effort
There's a love from me to you.

As long as life is loving
And gifts come from the heart,
Christ is still in Christmas
If we but live our part.

Christmas On Your Mind

Is Christ on your mind this Christmas

In the real old fashioned way –

Thinking of Him and His mission

When He came that Winter Day?

Is Christ in your thoughts this Season

As you hurry from store to store?

Is He the reason you're giving

And sharing more and more?

If so, His purpose is working

He always would wish it so

Keep Christ on your mind this Christmas

The thought that makes Christmas glow!

Christmas Picture

Paint our Christmas calm this year
Without a wreath or bell,
Paint it soft and quiet
With hoping, peace to tell.

Paint it gently with a love,
We've known so many years –
Of courage, strength and kindness
And smiles through all our tears.

Paint this year's Season grateful
For the past ones we have had;
The ones with brightest tinsel;
The ones that were so glad.

No matter how the painting
May look from time to time,
There'll always be a Christmas
With a sweet and tender chime.

So we will keep this Christmas
Framed with a loving glow,
And hope yours will be happy
Painted pure as glistening snow!

Christmas Replacement

We hung on the wall the little red sled,

Though it still is bright and new –

For the dear little boy who loved it

Just naturally grew and grew.

So a bigger sled is under the tree

To be an important part,

Of a bigger boy who grew so fast

But still has a little boy heart!

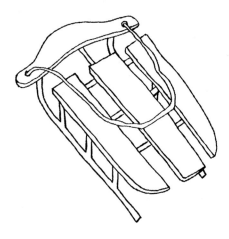

Christmas Snuggles

Memories grow sweeter
As Christmas thoughts grow near,
Reviving gold reflections
We have shared year after year.

Bright as morning sunshine
Sparkling on the snow,
Our hearts are renewed always
With the love we try to show.

Christmas is a choice of God
Made for one and all,
Beginning many years ago
In a lowly stable stall.

So have a "Snuggable" Christmas
In a "Huggable, Lovable," way,
Like the wishes I am sending
This Millennium Christmas Day!

Christmas Stocking Stuffer

Winter whispers "Christmas"
as the cold nips hand and toes,
and we brush the drifting snowflakes
from a red and tingly nose.

The green of summer's sweetness
is dressed in glistening white,
and the children's gleeful snow play
echoes day and night.

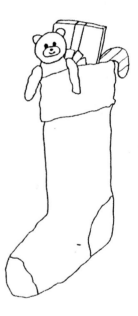

Christmas trees are lighted
and gifts appear beneath,
while our door is speaking "Welcome"
with Noel's timely wreath.

But when you hang your stockings,
reserve the biggest one
to be filled with joy and laughter
and loads of family fun.

The Master in His wisdom
gives us heaps of love to share,
so stuff that big old stocking
knowing He and I still care.

Stuff it full with all good wishes
of love and hope and health.
May this be your Christmas blessing
and your greatest Christmas wealth.

Christmas 2001

Christmas This Year

A Babe in a stable
With a Mother's sweet touch
A Father's protection;
A Son loved so much!

A child of great wisdom
Who came to be,
A Teacher of Goodness
For you and for me.

As a Man---for three years
Who walked on Life's road,
Then took on our burdens,
Our sins, as His load.

So Christmas is always
A time to recall,
Christ's greatest Blessings
To one and to all.

May the Season for you
Be as joyful and dear,
As the memories we share
Year after year.

You are close in my heart
As time edges away
And deepens my love,
On this Christmas Day!

1968

Christmas Time

How NEAR to the crowds is Christmas

As they hurry along the street?

Is it the fleeting shopping days

That cause their hustling feet?

How CLOSE to the crowds is Christmas?

Is it measured, in weeks or days,

By the number of gifts to purchase

In urgent, careless ways?

How DEAR to the crowds is Christmas?

For all, is it deep within?

Open Christ's door each Christmas---

Make room and keep room for Him!

Christ's Birthday

Let's remember a babe in a manger---

A Bethlehem stable of old,

How angels appeared to the shepherds

And to them the good tidings told.

Let's remember the light that shone brightly

…In hearts it must shine today.

Like the star that guided the Wise men,

It still can show us the way.

Let's remember the birthday of Jesus,

And let's keep it as sacred as then---

Let's remember to keep Christ in Christmas,

He came to bring peace to all men.

Graduating

Out of the learned Halls of Knowledge,
Going in to the fields of fame---
There's no need to fret about scoring
If you watch how you play the game.

Wisdom can well be your bases;
And courage, the bat filled with vim,
Though you will be your own pitcher,
Ambition will help you to win.

Use the ball of truth and kindness,
With a firm strong will, make it soar;
Have Christ as your umpire, always,
And many a "home run" you'll score.

Take time out when rest is needed,
Time out for a change in play;
And remember, time for the Master
Is the best-spent time of the day.

So play Life's game as you meet it.
Have faith in all things that you do.
Smile if you win---smile if you lose;
And your best will always come through.

Happy Holidays
Christmas Report 1967

Occupation

Elden---Jack of all Trades

Dorothy---Dough Dobber

Work---Repulsive

Health---Complaining

Weight---Heavy

Appearance---Lousy

Speed---Slower

In spite of these and old Arthur (itis)

And everything else he can do,

We'll have a real Merry Christmas

And are hoping you will, too!!

Merry Christmas

Happy Holidays 1993

If good wishes tied with ribbons

    Glisten bright with tinsel, too,

In boxes big and little,

    Wrapped in red and green or blue.

If all have lovely streamers

    To cheer you through the days;

Sprinkled with the stars of laughter

    And happiness to light your way.

If your tree is filled with patience,

    Branches thick with trims of joy;

If Peace and love abounding

    Mingle there among the toys,

If your Christmas fun with Family

    Is polished, too, with friends so dear –

Our wishes have been granted

    For your Holidays this year!

Holiday Thoughts

Butterflies have taken wing,

No more I hear the robins sing;

Jack Frost has been here with his Art---

Reminding me of Winter's start.

I close my eyes in peaceful dreams

Recalling joyful Christmas scenes,

The ones with "Little Pitty Pats,"

A puppy, and cute kitty cats.

Such happy years and Holidays

Fill memories a million ways,

Each has their very special own

Engraved on heart, as if in stone.

Each year I have sweet Christmas thoughts

Beyond the list of gifts I've bought---

There's all of you I love so much,

So "Greetings" with this Christmas touch!!

    Merry Christmas!

        God loves you

            And so do I.

July Fourth 1776 – 2003

Beat the drums and blow the horns
With fireworks in the sky,
Freedom day for the U.S.A.
Is still the Fourth of July.

And this is your dear Country
So fly the flag above
Wave it now and save it now,
Hold it with your love.

Long ago our soldiers fought
Democracy to gain,
So still be proud and shout it loud
Honor it the same.

Don't change it now to satisfy
Perhaps the whims of few.
Keep it free for you and me,
Fly the old red, white, and blue.

Celebrate with thankful hearts
Tradition should not fall,
Enjoy the things that freedom brings,
While there's happiness for all!

Love at Christmas

Christ reigns o'er our Christmas season

With each sparkling card we send,

He's in every tiny folder

That goes from friend to friend.

He's in every gift-wrapped package

From the largest to the small…

For in giving without loving

Gifts are no gift at all.

So a little bit of Heaven

Leaves and enters every heart,

With each gift and greeting

The Holidays impart!

Merry Christmas 1995

Howdy Folks! It's us again
Another year slipped by.
We don't know how it came and went
But Christmas now is nigh.

We didn't gain in knowledge,
...or forgot it if we did---
But one thing sure and certain
That "stuff" we can't keep hid.

It shows up somehow daily
But we laugh and struggle through,
Most folks are understanding
'Cause they have that trouble, too!

No matter if the days and weeks
Turn into months and years,
And each one adds a little
To our aches and pains and tears.

We'll still remember good times,
And fun times we once knew,
With those we love and cherish
...Good folks and friends like you.

We hope 'mid bows and ribbons
And gifts beneath your tree,
Christ's love will shine among them
For your heart to feel and see.

We wish you "Merry Christmas"
In that plain old fashioned way,
May your sock be filled with memories
Like ours, on Christmas Day!!

My Valentine Family

My life is full of sweetness

And my heart is filled with mirth,

For God has blessed me greatly

With my family here on earth,

SO

Roses may be red

And violets may be blue,

But there isn't any maybe

When I say that "I love you!"

October's Fun Time

Halloween is in the air,

With Spooks and Goblins everywhere.

Jack-o-Lanterns light their way,

For Ghosts don't come in light of day!

They hit the streets at eventide

In search of folks where treats abide.

They look for sweets and witches brew,

Red apples, gum and popcorn, too.

Their tastes are varied, that's for sure,

But they prefer the food that's pure.

So watch for Goblins---black or white---

Spooks to scare you in the night,

Black Cat shadows on the wall

Creepy masks for large and small.

They're sure to be about and seen

When night appears on Halloween!

Our Christmas Story

Christmas came to us this year with the same old chime of childhood heard every Christmas; "Daddy, when will you get our tree? Daddy, will you bring it in today? Please do!"

Daddy always comes to our rescue with the best that nature provides. Sometimes it's a small tree and sometimes it's a bit on the branchy side, but always there's an evergreen from the nearby fields or store to bring happiness to two lively little girls.

This year there was evidence our tree had brought happiness to someone else before it came to our household, for neatly set among its green pines was a tiny little brown nest. Daddy, being an admirer of birds did not disturb this home, but left it as a part of the decorations for his family to enjoy.

Shortly after the beauty of the Holiday Festivities had passed by, Mom removed the tree from its nook in the living room and carried it outside to be taken away with the other unwanted accumulations of the past month. On its way out however, the little nest became disengaged from its resting place and fell to the ground just outside our porch door. That evening, the seven-year old came in from chores with this bit of bird architecture grasped tightly in chubby fingers; "Look Mommy, I want to keep this always -- it is so sweet."

It sets in our window today. I notice a long black horsehair protruding in a huge loop above the tiny round circle woven of dried grass and sticks which must have been a precious home built by parents for their children, even as we provide homes for our own.

So in the words of our seven year old, "It is sweet," don't you think?

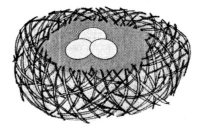

Season's Wishes

Recycle this…recycle that…

Paper, plastic, tin.

We're busy tossing many things

In exactly the right bin.

And so we're tossing wishes

Directed straight to you---

Recycled…"Merry Christmas"

And may happy dreams come true!

Thanksgiving Day

Over the turnpike, around the towns
To Grandmother's house we go...
The road points the way, for our new Chevrolet
As Dad safely drives through the snow.

The kids are excited and noisy
Thanksgiving at Grandpa's is great!
There'll be goodies galore, homemade by the score,
"Hurry Dad, let's don't be late!"

We'll be met at the door by Grandpa
And Grandma with kisses of joy,
Such Thanksgiving Cheer! It's a great time of year
For all little girls and boys.

Grandma stretches the table
To make room for her hungry bunch.
There's turkey and ham, plus big golden yams,
Her prize for a big "Super Lunch."

There's special noodles and dressing
Salads piled fluffy and high,
Cranberries too, for her hungry crew,
Baked apples and Pumpkin pie!

But wait...there's a Golden silence
For Grandpa's dear grateful prayer,
On this special day, we want him to pray...
He knows how to make us all care.

He is thankful for everyone present
And for every sweet moment each day...
For harvest of field and the bountiful yield
That brings us together to pray...

He remembers our Maker with honor
For showers of blessings each day
His thanks he imparts, straight from the heart
A message for all to obey.

The silence is once again broken
As Uncle John clears his throat,
We all join in, with our grateful "Amen"
And the eating begins on that note!!

Oh for Thanksgiving Day!!!

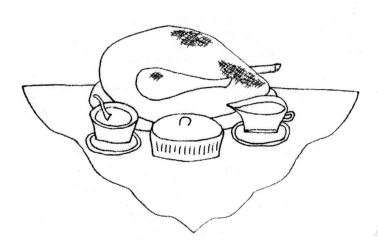

The Plane Truth

Dear Santa has traveled for many a year,
With a sleigh full of toys and cute reindeer,
Over mountains and housetops he's gone near and far,
And childhood's sweet memory we never must mar.

Today, Dasher his reindeer, is "Braniff" instead,
"United" is Dancer, could rightly be said;
There's "Ozark" replacing old Prancer this day,
And Vixen is taken by "T.W.A."

There's "Eastern" for Comet---Santa travels in style
And relaxes completely for mile after mile;
"Continental" lets Cupid stay home in the barns,
While "Delta" for Donder flies over the farms.

Blitzen no longer must leave his warm stall
For "Pan Am" will manage his part of the haul;
Rudolph reposes with red nose so bright,
While "Frontier" takes over, with Santa in flight.

On a crisp, snowy evening when Christmas is near,
Just listen now children, you surely can hear
Old Santa with orders he's bound to proclaim,
To the Pilots on duty of each Christmas plane.

"Up Braniff, United, and T.W.A.,
Ozark, we're ready, let's get on the way;
Up Eastern, Continental, to the sky we must take,
Come there now, Delta, we've a schedule to make!"

"Up Pan Am, up Frontier, over everything tall,
Let's fly-away, fly-away, fly-away all."
Then in an instant you'll hear him exclaim,
"Merry Christmas to all!"---as he boards his plane.

Yes, Santa still travels over snow-covered vales,
Above housetops and chimneys, through clouds he now sails
And this year, we'll join him on a Southern-bound jet,
For a Christmas in Georgia with our younger set.

And if you have missed him, just take it from us,
Old Santa no longer goes sleigh, car or bus,
He's traveling the airways and wants you to hear,
"Merry Christmas to all, and to all a good year!"

1999

Valentine Day Blues

Twinkle, Twinkle Ruby Star

How I wonder where you are?

First on land, and then in air---

It's not travel---its just where??

Mountain lodge was great, I bet;

Ski trips with the younger set,

Royal blood too, touched your hand

…Daughter of Samoa land.

So twinkle on, where 'ere you are

Chasing rainbows from afar.

May their light reflect a hue

Bringing love and joy to you.

FOLKS

A Mother's Fancy

My, how our hearts will flutter!
You know that we'll be proud
When we first present our baby
To our friends who 'round us crowd.

We know she'll be so very cute
That everyone will say,
"The sweetest baby that I've seen
For many and many a day."

She'll be such a little darling
With wisps of golden hair,
And tiny little fingers
That wiggle here and there.

Perhaps some peach-pink wrinkles,
Endearing dimples, too,
And curling long, dark lashes
Enclosing eyes of blue.

Two precious lips of softest pink
To pucker when she cries,
Or spread in smiles of sunshine---
For us a paradise!

There'll be features like her mother's;
Perhaps a stubby nose;
And maybe she will even have
Her daddy's crooked toes.

Oh, the fancies that we mother's have,
While we wait with wondering joy...
Why, maybe---yes, she just might be
Our own dear little boy!

Absent Love

The old porch swing is idle
    Moved only by the breeze,
That sings a lonely rhythm
    Through the empty bough of trees.

They too, seem sad without you
    As does the vacant chair,
Though time goes on forever
    We have never ceased to care.

The lawn is kept by others
    When velvet green appears.
Your evergreens grow profusely
    And I trim them through my tears.

The roses by the driveway
    Where we placed them side by side,
Burst there with fragrant memories
    My aching heart can't hide.

I miss you always, darling,
    As days' beauty turns to night
But your spirit lives beside me---
    Helps me through my worldly flight.

Aloha

It's been so nice to really know
Some super folks like you,
So good to have you as our friends
To do the things you do.

It's been so nice our paths have met
And crossed from day to day,
We're sure our lives have been enriched
Because you passed our way.

And though we lose, since you must go
There's much for which we're glad;
For others, we are sure, will reap
The same rewards we've had.

And you should know, since you're so wise
The reason you must go…
God wants your sunshine somewhere else,
And He has willed it so!

Anniversary

I tumble down the Hill of Memory---

A steep hill.

You were there

Always.

We ascended together

Over rough stones

Laughing.

You
> like the hope of Spring to a tired Winter
> the summer moisture to a thirsty Earth.

Certain
> as the Autumn harvest after ripening grain.

Quiet and peaceful
> as the first flakes of snow.

Fulfilling dreams and expectations.

Today the Plateau nears.

Hand in Hand

Grasping moments.

Summer, Autumn, Winter, Spring,

How swiftly they too ascend!

Bringing Hope, Promise, Peace and Love

Like you.

Anticipation

"Grandma, I'm getting playthings,"
A little voice declared.
A sparkle came to brown eyes---
His love he always shared.

I felt the great importance
Of words and eager eyes.
I knew that more would follow,
But I expressed surprise!

I longed for more discussion
Since Holidays were near...
Thinking that I needed help
For gifts that should appear.

But I learned very quickly,
His childish sweet desire
Already was projected
And I need not inquire.

He added quite emphatically
With grin, and then a pause---
"A choo-choo train I'm getting...
And it's from Christmas Claus!"

for Preston

Baby Touches

Hug me mommy

Hold me mommy,

Have a talk with me.

I listen mommy,

Hear you mommy

    Love I feel, and see.

Softly mommy

Gently mommy

Tell me, so I'll know

You're really mine

And I am yours

    We love each other so!

November 27, 1985

Barefoot Doll

(apologies to Barefoot Boy)

Blessings on thee, little maid,
Barefoot doll---pink cheeks won't fade.
With thy snow white pantaloons
And thy wakening midnight tunes,
You will soon dad's mistress be...
Keep right on crying, you shall see.
Soon he'll rock and warm your milk,
Lay you then on pillowed silk;
He'll get sleepy---may get cross,
But you'll get that extra toss.
Never mind, he's proud for sure,
See how much he can endure!

Blessings on thee, what a child!
Grandpa, Grandma will be wild,
You're lucky Babe that they are near,
With them around you need not fear.
Soon they, too, your slave shall be
Singing lullabies to thee.
Their hearts will pound with loving thumps,
And you'll keep them on the jump---
Just a squeal, a squirm, a twist,
Wiggle on, you'll soon get kissed!
You won't be spoiled; it can't be done,
But you'll all have lots of fun.
Come now---your blessings are complete,
With dad and mom and folks so sweet,
You're Queen of all, so blessings be,
To you and all your family!

Congratulations

As wedding bells ring out today

      With all their grandest chimes,

May they echo through your future

      And bring you best of times.

Each peal a golden tinkle

      Of love sincerely meant;

Together may they bring you

      Good luck and sweet content.

May chimes that bring you gladness

      Repeat from day to day;

And trials but faintly touch you,

      As you wend along Life's way.

Ambition always with you

      Each other as your guide---

You're bound for great successes,

      As you travel side by side.

for Bob and Vera, 1942

Dear Friends

No friends as nice as our friends

    And no friends more true blue,

Few friends do the lovely things

    That just ours seem to do.

So we'll remember through the years,

    And carry in our heart

A special place for our dear friends

    Who make friendship an art!

Equality

There's a stage of one's life quite distasteful

To those whose company we share,

To us it's a phase that's perfected…

To our friends…it's one they can't bear.

For rarely do friends enjoy grandparents'

Gloating or bragging of heirs.

Remember, your friends are your own age---

Your grandkids---no better than theirs!

Eulogy to Mother

Hers were the riches of kindness,

She had not a wealth of fame,

But she gave of herself for others---

To love and to serve was her aim.

Hers was the touch of an angel;

God knew it and spared her so long.

…for us an example of goodness,

Showing us right from wrong.

Hers was the work of the Master;

She tended her flock every day,

She was "our Mom" and "our Grandma"

We loved her---God keep her, we pray.

December 26, 1966

Extended Love

She came to us in April
At the precious age of nine,
With a sparkle like the dewdrops
In the wake of sweet springtime.

Her eyes are clear and pretty,
Like a crystal pool of blue.
She is nimble as a kitten
And as playful as one, too.

She loves the open spaces…
Daddy's tools her greatest toys;
And she brought a slice of sunshine
That has multiplied our joys.

As years roll on in numbers
And she leaves childhood behind,
May she cherish happy moments
That we hope to help her find!

for Kim

Favorite Guests

Wee Miss "Mustn't Touch It"
And brother "I Will Do"
Have come to stay at Grandpa's
For a day or two.

Little "Mustn't Touch It"
Doesn't miss a touch,
And brother "I Will Do"
Does about as much!

Drawers are standing open
Where those on tippy toes,
Peek to see what Grandma
Keeps higher than their nose.

Big and little splatters
Across the kitchen floor,
Cookie crumbs and sugar
Lead to every door.

A chair to reach the faucet
Is pushed beside the sink,
Where little hands are cleaned
"Most quicker than a wink."

One would like Lasagna---
The other---"Pizza, please."
Both would like a Pepsi.
Requests just never cease.

Lollipops---all flavors,
Ice cream on a stick,
Are always found at Grandpa's...
Good with every lick.

Cherry pie for breakfast??
Unheard of before now,
"just this once" at Grandma's;
"O jeepers, that's a Wow!"

What a joyful blessing
These two can bring about,
Busy, busy, busy---
But fun, without a doubt!

for Jason & Kaycee

First Grandchild

There's a roly-poly duck in the ferris wheel,
    Three blocks and a speckled bug;
A paper sack for a Howdy hat,
    And cookie crumbs over my rug.

There's a little green pail with handle removed,
    Two spools and a ball or two;
A little cloth book with a kitty cat,
    And a string pulled out of my shoe.

There's an empty box with a nibbled top,
    And a soft little squeegee dog
To make for contentment of one tiny Miss
    Who at Grandpa's can stir up a fog!

She pushes the footstool any old place,
    And bangs on the walls and the chairs;
She plays in the cupboards, the pots and the pans
    Or anywhere else that she cares.

Although she is pampered and humored and spoiled,
    She's our tiny blue-eyed queen;
And she seems to be the only Grandchild
    That Grandma ever has seen.

for Syndi

First Lady

Jackie belonged to our Nation
With an aura of grandeur and hope.
She quieted the spirits of people
When she opened her heart and spoke.

Her voice was known to millions,
Dispensed with a rich mellow tone---
A wisp of a whisper delivered
As she poured out her message alone.

A message of strength and endurance
When we mourned a leader of men,
And her loss was even greater;
A husband, a father and friend.

With tender, gentle persuasion
When adversity touched her life,
She lived an example of courage
In her time of deep pain and strife.

And now she belongs to the ages,
"First Lady"---with her noble esteem
Having served her family and country
With a love that was pure and serene.

September, 1994

For a Friend

God sent a friend along my way
To clasp my hand and by me stay,
And always when her help was asked
She faltered not, though big the task.

She sweetly lived---this friend of mine.
Thus 'round my heart a love entwined.
And though God took her soon away,
Her love lives on with me today.

I now shall say my path is bright
Because she lived and left her light.
A better someone I will be
Since she once walked along with me.

I'll wish that I might pass along
Her smiling ways, her happy song,
So others too, might better be,
That she once lived---a friend to me!

Friends

Sometimes it's almost awesome

Through life's span of crooks and bends

How strangers' paths are mingled

And they become dear friends.

And so it was in gray-hair years

We met with common touch,

Our hearts were joined in music

An art we loved so much!

But greatest common interest

We share that binds our tie,

Is our Lord in all His goodness—

Love and mercy from on High.

Grandpa and Grandma

It's awfully nice to be Grandpa
To a brand new little boy;
To think of the ways you can spoil him
By giving him every toy.

Soon he will tag after Grandpa
And learn how to hammer and saw;
Know all the wires in a T.V.,
And all the electrical law.

But nicer than being Grandpa,
(Though he would never concede)
Is being a little boy's Grandma
And knowing a Grandson's need.

For Grandma will love and rock him
And sing him sweet lullabies,
She'll soothe away all his troubles
By cuddling him when he cries.

O yes, it's great to be Grandpa
And great to be Grandma, too---
Just spoil him and love him and treasure
Each moment his whole life through.

Grandpa's Old Porch Swing

We have such fun at Grandpa's
Out on the old porch swing,
Where Grandpa sits and reads to us
And sometimes even sings.

He tells us little stories
About common folk and kings;
And all the while we're listening,
Back and forth he swings.

There's shrubs and vines and flowers
That grow along the walk,
And busy bees that hustle…
Grandpa shows us as he talks.

The hummingbirds, he tells us,
Sip nectar on the wing,
And if we're really quiet
We might see them from the swing.

He sometimes speaks of Grandma,
How they courted in the spring
And cuddled in the moonlight
On her father's old porch swing.

At laughs and love and spoiling
Our Grandpa is a whiz;
And he's touched us all with kindness,
…These five grandkids of his.

And the greatest of our treasures
As we think of childhood things
Will be the times with Grandpa
Out on the old porch swing.

Honorable Mention

To be able to walk with a king and know

                              that I am someone;

To be able to walk in the same shoes

                           with a man who

fixes the furnace,

mows the lawn,

Keeps the gas tank full,

and know that

               I am still someone;

To be able to hear his laugh,

know his wisdom,

see his smile,

And to know that I am the object of these---

               All are a part of my being me!

Maybe he is not a king in other's eyes;

Maybe he doesn't repair your furnace,

cut your grass,

or pay your bills.

Maybe you don't see his grin,

hear his voice,

   or agree with me in any way---

But to me, he is my world,

the father of my children,

the man I love,

And that's what makes this,

As well as every other day

  A Happy Father's Day at our house

How about yours??

Legacy

She never won an Oscar
Nor an Emmy in her life;
She wasn't Miss America
Or the President's young wife.

She never made big speeches
Or wore diamonds and fur;
Her attire was plain and simple,
The frills were not for her.

She never crossed the ocean
Or traveled on the planes;
She didn't drive an auto---
Seldom held the horses' reins.

She didn't like rough speaking,
Nor loud and useless talk.
She soothed her trials with calmness
Derived from a garden walk.

She craved no admiration;
Her gain was love she won
By giving---always giving
More than she should have done.

She loved sweet song and rainbows,
Wild geese in patterned flight,
The hum of happy voices
From morning's dawn 'til night

She liked returning robins
When the April Showers play,
And heard the first frogs croaking
With the early warm spring day.

Her winters were not dreary;
With her needles and her thread,
No time for idle rocking.
Few books she ever read.

She loved her old piano,
Nimble fingers skimmed the keys;
Sweet "MUSIC TO REMEMBER"
She made with greatest ease.

She made our home a castle
With her tender golden touch,
While she wove a web of kindness
'Round those she loved so much.

She was my angel mother,
And many more must be
Just like this "Mom" of my life
And the memory she left me.

Little Artist

We have a little artist
Who works from morn 'til late,
He uses for his palette
The sugar bowl or plate.

He may have for his canvas
My whitest table spread,
Or sometimes, if I'm busy
He may just use my bed.

His colors are most different,
At mixtures he's a dream---
His work is not his worry---
He has no color scheme.

His oils are cake and butter,
Or beans and corn and peas,
Potatoes, gravy, pancakes,
Or other foods like these.

But, oh, the things he covers
With sweet and sticky muss.
Sometimes he even colors
The furniture…and us.

His brushes---tiny fingers
Dipped deeply here and there
In every bowl he reaches,
While I grab everywhere!

Sometimes he uses others:
A knife, or daddy's spoon.
But always he's a painter
At morning, night, or noon.

His pictures are so priceless...
In love's gallery they will stay
For he's our little artist.
Has he ever been your way?

for Dennis

Little Bride Dolly

Little Bride Dolly
On a high closet shelf,
You look oh-so-lonely
Up there by yourself.

You haven't seen sunshine
For ages it's true,
And you're ever so quiet
The endless hours through.

Do you wish for the darling
Who loved you so much,
And cuddled you daily
With a mother's soft touch?

She tenderly wrapped you
And put you away
Before changing her name
On that fall wedding day.

Your gown of white satin,
Lace trim of the same
Has long ago yellowed,
As well as your train.

There's a box there beside you
With another trousseau.
It, too, is white satin
With a yellow-aged bow.

Your brown curly tresses
Untouched for so long,
Are as she caressed them
With a lullaby song.

She hasn't forgotten
She put you up there
In her own little closet,
Now empty and bare.

But I move you gently
When trying to clean.
If you should cry, "Mama"
I know I would scream.

She doesn't surmise,
Little Dolly so dear,
She left us fond memories
When she left you here.

Lone little loved one,
She cares for you still;
And some day she'll claim you,
I'm sure that she will.

We're happy she's happy…
'Though sometimes we're blue.
For, Little Bride Dolly,
We miss her, too.

Little Chums

Down the street together
Holding hand in hand,
Go the Kindergarten Lady
And the Kindergarten Man.

Side by side as neighbors
They lived for five long years,
And now it's time for study---
Bless the little dears!

She wears a dress of ruffles
Swished with lace can-can,
Blue jeans and pull-on sweater
Bedecks the little man.

Her pony tail of yellow
Dances here and there,
While red accents his crew cut---
They're modern---this young pair!

He brushes back her tear drops,
Caused by a faulty jump.
She pats and speaks so gently
As she patches up his bumps.

Together they're a picture
Complete in every way...
This Kindergarten couple
Who pass by every day.

Lonesome

Miss our front porch swinging

    When the sun gets low,

Miss our friendly chatter

    More than you'll ever know.

Miss those little visits

    Across the backyard fence,

And soppy tears together

    That seldom make much sense.

Miss your words of wisdom,

    The courage you bestow;

Miss your deeds of kindness

    And your happy glow.

Miss your ray of sunshine,

    Miss your loving touch;

Miss you . . . Gee, I miss you,

    You'll never know how much!

Mama's Aprons

Our Mama wore an apron,
Did your mama wear one, too?
Made from calicos and ginghams,
And feed sacks flowered blue?
Each apron had a pocket
Often trimmed with tape or lace,
Or a bit of bright embroidery
For those worn a special place.
She cut them from the patterns
She first made with utmost care,
Making scallops, points and ruffles,
Varied styles she liked to wear.

When the lamplight shadows gathered,
She brought out the old machine
To treadle it for stitching
Each new apron's basted seam.
And when the seams were finished
And the kitchen stove was hot,
She heated the old flat irons
To press smooth each wrinkled spot.
How lovely were the aprons
That our mother made and wore,
Keeping always neat and tidy
As she did each daily chore.

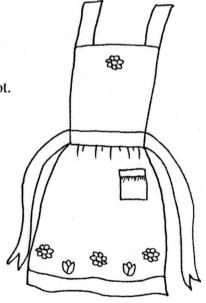

Mistaken Identity

A smile,

A greeting,

Some talk,

Then friends.

A trust,

Confiding---

Deepening trends.

Broken vows,

A hurt,

More talk,

Then, it ends.

Only

People,

Never friends!

Mom

Dear Mom;

> If you could go
>> where in our dreams we'd have you be,
>
> Could you e'er guess that by our side a Righteous path you'd
> help us see?

Gee Mom;

> If you could have
>> all that our hearts would want you to,
>
> Your blessings would be greater than stars at night that dot the
> blue.

And Mom;

> If you could know
>> the loves that think of you each day,
>
> T'would make your heart lighten with every care that's blown
> your way.

So Mom;

> If e'er it seems
>> that those you love forget to do their part . . .
>
> Remember – they will ne'er forget – for you are always in our
> hearts.

Mother's Hands

What do you say to a Mother's Hands
That have worked the long years through,
Weaving a delicate web of love
Around the whole heart of you?

What can you say when they're worn with care?
…Only you know their real worth---
They're the most precious of all the hands
That labor upon the earth.

What will you say when they're folded white
On a breast that's silent and still?
Alas! It will be too late for praise
So give it now if you will.

Press them close to your own warm lips
And hold them with tender care,
And thank her now for all they have done…
For love they willingly share.

And even if words just don't unfold,

Hug her, and she'll understand.

Do it today. It will help to repay

The work of your Mother's hands.

Neighbors

Because of you our life has been
A treasure chest complete,
Filled brim to brim with happiness
That time will ne'er defeat.

Because of you, through heavy tears
Our hearts have eased a bit,
And we have learned not all big things
Are those that make the hit.

For years our lives have intertwined,
We've traveled many a road.
Up hill and down o'er all the bumps
We've shared each other's load.

We would not have the world believe
Our skies were always blue,
We've had our trials but each forgave
As always good friends do.

We cannot live a million years---
But should God grant us to,
We'd want our house next door to yours
Neighbors...because you're you!

Nephew

Little footsteps, tiny hands,
A "Beanie Cap" with trim.
An impish smile but loving arms –
    We remember him!

Sparkling eyes, a neat young man
With happy fun-based whims,
Yet special warmth for all mankind –
    We remember him!

A Doctorate in Philosophy
And Science, worked with vim,
A father, brother, teacher, son –
    We remember him!

A life so full for life itself,
He loved both friend and kin,
He taught us each with deep insight –
    We remember him!

Conrad Noel Bensyl
September 19, 1937 – June 10, 1989

Our Baby

He picked a blossom as he passed,
And put it to his nose,
The petals dropped, when gently touched,
And fell on dimpled toes.

He stooped to pick the fragments
From tiny feet so bare,
But oh, the breeze was quicker,
The petals were not there.

So then he plucked another,
It, too, a pansy gay,
And offered it to puppy
Who shook its head in play.

That lovely bed of flowers
Two precious blossoms lost;
But it flowered still in sunshine
And did not mind the cost.

And as he toddled onward
Toward greater things to see,
We wished he might forever
Find all his world so free.

Our Daughters

God put the stardust in your eyes,
The sunlight in your hair;
He gave you riches in your smiles
Few others can compare.

He gave you beauty of the rose
That only mothers see.
And added angel sweetness
For His touch of ecstasy.

He made you pure as lilies white,
Brim full of poise and grace,
And then He dropped in hope and faith---
God leaves no empty space.

He gave you skill in all you do,
Your work, your joy, your play,
And each of these He gave to you
In His own special way.

But of all these things He did so well
Without one bit of fuss,
He finished with the nicest one
And gave you each to us!

Our Little Folks Next Door

She's one of God's wee angels
Who touch the hearts of all.
She's here and there and yonder
Within her mother's call.

She brings crumpled letters
In tiny crumpled hands---
With crayon marks and colors
Postmarked from unknown lands.

She may bring small tomatoes,
Hand picked in tiny pail---
Then sweetly gives her neighbors
With smiles that never fail.

"Nuff?" she quizzes softly
As she hands them one by one,
And two big eyes of crystal blue
Flash clearly---share my fun!

She's protected by big brother
Whose age is only four.
They're such a precious couple
---These little Folks next door!

for Becca & Tad, August 1994

Our Ruby

She lived in a house at the end of a lane,

    Where many dear friends came to call,

And each was a favorite friend to her,

    For she loved not a few – but all.

Her hands ever busy with needles and thread,

    She shared with the young and the old,

All of the treasures created by her,

    More precious than silver or gold.

The little white house will be lonely and sad,

    Where the once busy lane still ends,

She was our Mother, our Grandma and Sister,

    Auntie and Neighbor and Friend.

July, 1987

Ours to Hold

Could we have picked from story book

A babe with soft angelic look;

A doll with mischief in her eyes

And smile direct from paradise;

A tiny fairy, cute and sweet,

From curl on top to dimpled feet;

We could have turned the pages through

And never found one dear as you!

for Kaycee

Pap-Paw's Shadow

Grandpa has a shadow.
It's only just so high,
And it tags him always---
---This active little guy.

This shadow is quite different
Because it has a voice,
And asks a million questions
Pap-paw answers without choice.

He's just a baby shadow---
You know he's only two;
But he's right after Grandpa
In all he tries to do.

This little blonde-haired image
'Most gets hid sometimes
'Mid all the workshop's clutter
Where they work with oak and pine.

But sometimes he wanders
Chasing butterflies and bugs---
And then he's back to Grandpa
When he needs protective hugs.

He asks Pap-paw to "up it"
And carry him along,
When tagging makes him weary,
Or it's time for bedtime song.

So always when he's busy,
Or when Gramps takes a nap,
This shadow stays right with him…
Climbs right up in his lap.

It takes a heap of lovin'
To help childish hurts and heart;
But Grandpa knows the trouble
And mends the broken parts.

He's really kept quite busy
---Not with work, but play;
For he loves his little grandson,
Grandpa's shadow every day.

for Jeff

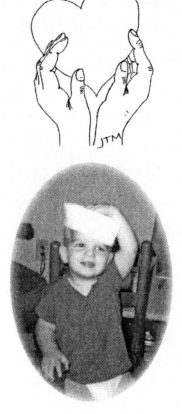

Possum Holler Wishes

Us old skunks in these here parts
    Have covered hills and woods,
Passin' round the story
    You jes' ain't feelin' good.

We've told the birds, they told the squirrels,
    The butterflies and bees.
We also told the chipmunks.
    We even told the fleas.

We've told the rabbits and the fox,
    The possum and the coon.
We've sent the word jes' everywhere.
    From earth to stars and moon.

And all of them with all of us
    Will shout across the sea,
When you are back in these here parts
    As frisky as can be!

Please, Grandma

Rock gently, Grandma
Soon baby will know
Your soft, loving touches
That cuddle him so.

Too soon he will change
From wee little tyke
To questions and tadpoles,
And worms and a bike.

To books and to lessons,
To football and track.
How soon, oh how soon
You will be looking back.

Remembering these moments
So precious and few,
Love him and rock him...
Please, Grandma, please do!

Related

She gathers up the fun things
Of the days that come and go,
And stores them in her memory
For the ones who love her so.

If she has any heartaches
Seldom others ever know,
She hides her cares and troubles
With a laugh that seems to grow.

Admired by those who know her
For the joy she always brings,
She lifts the low in spirits
And helps lonely hearts to sing.

Happiness Personified---
That's the way I list her!
I love her more than others---
She is my precious sister.

Romance 1953 – 2003

Down in Missouri where the whippoorwills call
And the goldenrod blossoms in early fall;
Where the wild rose fragrance fills the country air
And overcomes that Jimson weeds' haughty flair.

Where Prairie chicken humdrum is heard in the morn,
And the cows break the fences to get in the corn;
Where sometimes is heard the coyotes' howl
Joined by the sound of the old hoot owl

Where the bluebirds twitter from their fence post house.
And the cats never bothered a computer mouse!
Here dwells great people, young and old
Where love never changes---we have been told.

It was here in a college a couple found
Loves old story made the same old round.
He courted his lady in his kind of car,
And they motored around under twinkling stars.

The old moon winked with a big wide grin,
For he knew right away that love would win.
Soon came wedding bells---cupid doesn't miss---
They vowed to love always, 'til the moon and stars kiss.

Five little angels found this home to bless,
And strengthened the ties of happiness---
One little girl and four little guys
Completed this couple's paradise.

For Fifty years they have been side by side
Choosing the "Good Book" and God as their guide.
They have had a life of many good deeds,
Just helping others who have troubled needs.

That same old moon still winks from above
For he sees the two still fondly in love
Their kindness falls gently like the old moonglow
And warms the life of others---making hearts overflow.

Y'all have long been our Iowa Friends, too,
And we're so glad old Missouri gave us you.

Silver Wedding Day

Mom must have been a darling
When she caught our Daddy's eye;
So little, sweet and pretty
And quiet-like and shy.

She must have been so dainty
With her graceful winning way –
She must have been the sweetest,
So young and blithe and gay.

Dad must have seen how lovely
A person she would be,
To love and cherish always,
And to keep him company.

Mom must have also noticed
That our Dad was special too,
So handsome, wise and honest,
With a heart sincere and true.

He must have been "real swingin"
With his chuckle and sly grin –
Gentle, kind and charming,
When she fell in love with him.

Their love must have been special,
Unselfish, pure and deep,
The kind that's meant forever
Within two hearts to keep.

It must have been intended
That two like they should meet,
For theirs has been a marriage
With happiness complete.

So this anniversary
Your children want to say
"God bless you Mom and Daddy –
We love you more each day."

"May all your days be sunshine
Kissed only by the dew
And may your joys be doubled
And your wishes all come true."

Sixty Wedded Years

'Twas days of horse and carriage
When this young man thought of marriage,
And it was then he wooed his lady fair!
Though he didn't have a "fliver"
The lovin that he "give her"
Soon led unto a mighty happy pair.

Then Spring in all her glory
Helped him whisper loves old story,
A way back there in eighteen ninety four;
And their wedding vows were spoken,
Never ever to be broken...
As lasting as the wedding band she wore.

The stork in all his blindness
Brought them a special kindness
For prime perfection here he did contrive.
And when all his visits ended,
This couple had been befriended
With loving little bundles numbered five.

Life's path right then was scattered
With joys that never shattered,
For children made this cherished home complete;
And they battled stormy weather,
Always holding hands together,
Preparing for the trials they would meet.

Now sixty Gold years later,
He to this love still caters,
With tenderness no youth has ever known;
Though soft silver streaks her tresses,
He still lives for her caresses
And lovelight that her eyes have always shown.

So great has been their measure
Of friends and earthly treasure,
Since that Spring when first they said, "I do" –
God's gifts so richly tendered
Have ever been remembered,
His blessings building every day anew.

This Man

"By the sweat of the brow" he earned his way
Working the land in the heat of the day.
Morning and evening chores were done
As he labored between the up and down sun.
Never a complaint of injustice he claimed,
And for hardships he suffered, no one he blamed.
His horses and mules were always his pride,
His hunting dogs ever at his side…
        My dad was this man.

He was jovial and happy and yet he was stern;
Knew how to laugh and how to be firm.
He counted his friends by all whom he knew.
Many they were, and all ages too,
With all kinds of people he was at ease,
And tiny folks loved his ability to tease.
Harsh, you might say, if you didn't know,
But to me and my sister he had a warm glow.
        Our dad was this man.

He taught us the values we'd need in life;
How to meet disappointment and worldly strife.
Respect and honor he did demand,
But we learned these from a loving hand.
He was witty and wise and daily he read,
"To keep up with the world," he always said.
Strong in convictions, convincing, too;
"Never trouble trouble 'til trouble troubles you."
        Dad was this man.

Youngest Grandson

Little shoe marks on my floor,
   Little hand prints on my door,
      Cracker box with broken lid,
         Empty cookie jar I've hid.

Pots and pans are everywhere,
   Toys are scattered here and there.
      Beyond my feet out rolls a ball---
         Toy truck crunches, wheels and all!

Oh yes, he's been here, bless his heart,
   And oh, I miss him…tears now start,
      Little Grandson, precious one;
         Grandma loves this mess of fun!

Again tomorrow please come back…
   You make a mansion of this shack.
      When you are here this house to bless
         It is a castle of happiness.

for Jason

FUN

1920's Plumbing

There's a memory deep within us
That stirs our youthful mind,
Where the spiders and the crickets
We knew we'd always find.

Where the door was hooked or fastened
With a block of splintered wood,
And the creaky rusty hinges
Never worked just like they should.

A well-worn path of daily use
Wound through the grass and weeds.
A long, long way it sometimes seemed
To care for urgent needs.

The cats were always in the way
And those Banty roosters too,
---the ones prepared for battle
Every time they met with you.

The geese and guineas scattered
When they saw us on the run…
They knew that we meant business,
Wasn't out for play or fun.

At last amid the Hollyhocks
That stood so stately tall
We reached the door and hurried in,
Our private little stall.

Sometimes a lacy, silken web
Was swinging in that place,
And Mr. Spider's work we felt
Across our ashen face.

We always watched for "Skeeters"
And those angry honey "Bees,"
They never are particular…
They pop you where they please.

It seemed we shut the world outside
Yet always there within,
Was a stack of dusty catalogs
…No Charmin, soft and thin.

This dear old "House of Comfort"
Welcomed many an anxious guest.
It had no means for flushing,
But for us it was the best!!

Another Look At Shoes

We all know shoes are special
You've found that is true,
But who gives them credit
For all that they do?

They always are with you
And help WALK you through
A heart that is troubled
When you're feeling blue!

They are there when you laugh
And there when you cry,
Good shoes are our partners
We must not deny.

They come in all sizes,
Small---medium and large
Their prices are likewise
But...we pay the charge.

They range in all colors
From bright rainbow hues---
To black, brown and white---
---These things we call shoes.

There's high heels and low heels
And some we call slings.
There's run shoes, and fun shoes
For all sorts of things.

There's high tops and low tops
In boots we all wear,
For weather in Iowa
We each need a pair.

There's buckles and bow trims,
There's buttons and ties
---But changes in fashion
Dictate what we buy.

Our modest old shoes!
If they could just talk
And tell us their stories
They know from each walk!

Would your's be so blest
Each week they could say---
"We went to church Sunday
And I heard you pray?"

If shoes could start talking
Would they ALSO say
"I walked with an angel---
WE had a great day??"

Give thanks for footwear
And all that they do---
Be grateful, my friends
For the lowly old shoe!

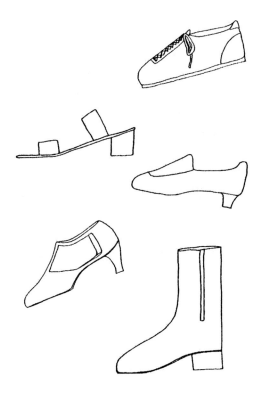

Balloon Days

We're all in a tizzy---
Excitement runs high,
It's time for the races.
Balloons in the sky!

Aunt Ruby is coming
With all of her joy,
And bringing her grandson
A fine teenage boy.

There are neighbors of hers
From old Kansas state,
And Missouri-good-friends
Who remembered the date.

And then our own family
Of wee folks and big,
We know will be here
To observe all the rig.

We'll be late to bed;
But early we'll rise
To see all the beauty,
Adrift in the skies.

We'll sip on hot coffee,
Cold pop or iced tea,
Between each ascension
We're eager to see.

We'll eat on the run
The sandwich and pie.
While stretching our necks
We'll be straining the eye.

We just can't describe
Our sheerest delight
Sharing with people
This colorful sight.

Each year when Man's rainbow
Appears o'er our town,
We want loved ones here
For the final countdown.

We hope they'll return
For attractions and fun,
'Til all the balloons
Hide away with the sun!

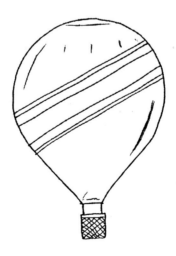

Candy Cane

I took a lick of my peppermint stick

And thought it tasted yummy.

It used to be on my Christmas tree,

But I like it better in my tummy!

Club Day

My mom she's in an awful state,

It's time for club---she's sure she's late!

Her hair is in an awful muss,

She growls and snaps and spats at us.

She made a sandwich and some tea

And called it dinner---oh dear me!

She's left her dishes all undone,

Puffs her nose while on the run.

She grabs her bag and off she spins,

While dad looks on and sort of grins.

For nothing else upsets mom's state

Like club day does when she is late!

Country Woman's Lament

Pea pickin', bean pickin',
Balin' the hay,
Corn plowin', chick raisin',
All in a day!

4-H and Bible school
Both to be taught;
Weddin' bells ringin',
As hostess I'm sought.

The washin', the ironin',
Laundry untold,
Pop's always hungry . . .
Three meals must unfold.

Grass needs a haircut,
And garden a hoe.
Bugs need a sprayin'
So taters can grow.

No use complainin',
All need to be done.
Wish I was two . . .
I'd have twice as much fun!

Dad's Discovery

I'm in the dog house...
    I tracked up her floor;
I got the wrong things
    When I went to the store.

I scattered my papers
    All over the place,
And left a moustache
    When I shaved my face.

I upset the ashtray
    And let in the dog,
Puffed on my cigarette
    And stirred up a fog.

I ate of her dinner---
    Said no word of praise,
But knew my mistake
    When I met her gaze.

The worst of my fumbles
    She'll never forgive,
Man oft "hangs himself"
    Though he still lives.

For I changed the T.V.
    And turned to the fights,
Then raved at the kids
    For lounging in tights.

My ultimate error
    Caused much more ado,
For I found out Mama
    Had leotards too!

Extravaganza

Blossom spent her pennies
When she went to the fair,
She really didn't spend them
On ribbons for her hair.

She bought some cotton candy
Drank lemonade and pop,
She ate popcorn and peanuts,
And rode the Spinning Top.

She had snow cones and pizza,
And a watermelon slice;
Hamburgers and some french fries
And a bit of orange ice.

She finished with a hot dog
And ice cream on a stick –
Too many ill-spent pennies
– For Blossom got real sick!

Have You Had It?

The flu bug will bite, if you don't watch out.
He picks on the weak as well as the stout.
You're feelin' okay, as light as a song,
When lo, in the night that bug comes along!
You freeze and you shake, and maybe you choke
But believe me, sir, he'll have a tight rope.
Hunt all the covers from attic to stair;
Turn up the furnace for lots of hot air.
You'll shake and shiver 'til you reach a boil
And then start swimming in body oil.
Got such a fever you're dying of thirst---
You start taking sips, each one is the worst.
Now it's your throat, can hardly swallow,
Or then it's your head---"wish it were hollow."
Next it's your back---You're sure it will break,
Nothing escapes him, for every spot aches.
The good old doctor does all that he can:
Prescribes the best drug that is known to man.
Down to the drug store for big yellow pills---
Reach for your wallet to cancel the bill.
You see the bottle and let out a screech!
The clerk says, "Mister, they're sixty cents each!"
Still that old flu bug is awful to lick,
Just take it from me, he's no country hick.
He's got all the latest with virus and stuff
And if he bites once, that sure is enough!

How To Serve A Five Course Meal To Ten In A Hot Air Balloon

First we will remember
      that space is scarce and small
For ten in a huge Gondola
      there must be food for all.

We'll start with juice or cocktails
      Your choice, served with a straw
And hors d'oeuvres from a basket
      which might be cooked or raw.

A piping cup of zesty soup
      we'd pass to each with care
And hope the airborne diners
      would like this party fare.

From Spacemen's borrowed menu
      We'll serve their special mix
Those "talked about" and energized
      dried beef or smoked meat stix.

To end this floating dining
      up there in a peaceful sky,
We'll serve a frozen Chocolate Malt
      and imagine it is pie!

I've Lost It

I've lost this and I've lost that,
I've lost my coat and lost my hat;
I've lost my shoes and lost my socks,
I've lost the keys that turn my locks.
I lost a recipe I like.
If I had one...I'd lose my bike.
I lost my pill box and my pills,
Lost all the stuff that helps my ills.

I lost my pencil and its pad,
Lost 'most everything I've had.
Lost a camera and its case...
Still have the flowers, but lost the vase.
Played with money, I shouldn't have done,
Lost two daughters, gained some sons.
But all in all, I hope I'll find
The last I lost...my crazy mind!!

Kitchen Notions

There's a gal who works in notions
At a counter by the door---
She's often cleaning celery
Or carrots by the score.

Sometimes she tosses salads,
Shreds the cabbage by the pound.
Opens gobs of pickle slices---
---Any kind that can be found.

She works in other items
Like kraut and corn and peas,
Sometimes she is most surrounded
By vegetables like these.

She counts pineapple slices
And spicy apple rings.
She is busy at her counter
With all these numerous things.

Her wares are really many
So that's why we can say,
"Our Mary works in notions,
A variety each day!"

Lines for Brother's Birthday Gift

This Camp Stool's for fishin'

Or sittin' and wishin'

Or it could be for weedin' as well.

It's fine for just shadin'

Right after spadin'

Or pickin' sweet berries in dell.

Whatever its status –

Please don't be mad at us,

We hope you will use it a spell.

Our Jersey Queen

Oh, for the life of our old Jersey cow.
She seems so contented as I see her now.
Slowly she moves to the foliage green
Pauses for water while crossing the stream.
All day she grazes o'er acres of ground,
While picking the best where best can be found.
There's timothy, clover and blue grass, too,
Sweet feed for old Bossy, none other will do!
In summer she's fed on choicest of grass;
In winter, a ration and hay that's first class.
Kept sheltered from wintry winds that blow;
Protected by vaccines from ills we know.
Then there is fly spray to help with her fight
Against flies and mosquitoes that are certain to bite.
Never complaining as she chews her cud;
With a life so pleasant, we wonder who would?

Yearly, with Bossy so deeply content
We eagerly wait for her Blessed Event.
For weeks she is handled with greatest care,
A special tending which seems only fair;
And when it's all over without a fuss…
We wonder who's proudest, old Bossy or us?

If there is admission at cow Heaven's Gate
And the Good Saint asks for her claim of fate---
As he hears her plea, puts her name in gold,
Like Abou Ben Adhem's (we have been told)
The name of Old Bossy will top them all,
And she'll walk forever in Pastures Tall.

Progress?

Yesterday's Grandmother when a small child,
Was accustomed to everything moderate and mild.
She woke in the morning and without mistake,
The first sound she heard was Pa shaking the grate.
The ashes and wood must be handled just right
To heat the old cookstove for biscuits so light.

Grandma would snuggle in covers piled high
'Til the teakettle whistled its good morning cry.
Then quickly she jumped to a cold wooden floor,
Tripped down narrow stairway and through kitchen door
To a steaming hot breakfast of oatmeal with cream,
Or biscuits and gravy with ham fresh and lean.

Presently, Grandchildren live a new way,
Their noises are different at the first break of day
A cycle zooms by and they open their eyes
To another new world of roaring Jet skies.
And then comes the ring of the Microwave
Mom's energy conscious---she's trying to save.

They toss back the sheet and jump to the floor
There is carpet from bedroom right through kitchen door
Then quickly they grab for a cold cereal bowl,
Or press oven button to warm a sweet roll.
Now which is the better we might ask of you
Dear Grandmother's day or her Grandchildren's view?

Reflection

I stepped into a hallway
And I met a stranger there.
She was tall and somewhat haggard,
Silver streaks were in her hair.

I thought she seemed quite startled
As I nodded with a smile.
'Though she returned the gesture,
Friendly didn't seem her style.

She quickly stepped and whispered,
"Excuse me, won't you please?"
But I only saw the movements
Of her lips so ill at ease.

For I too, was apologetic.
Then I realized with shame
I was looking in a mirror---
It was I who had no name.

Satisfaction

I haven't been to Frisco
  Nor seen Virginia's caves;
Nor have I scanned the seashore
  Or the great Atlantic waves.

A subway's out of question,
  Kate Smith I only hear;
A cruise and old Manhattan?
  Ah…music to my ear!

New York and all its grandeur
  Are fairy tales to me;
Black Hills and old Wyoming
  Are places yet to see.

My trips are short but frequent
  Between the house and barn,
Then out to tend the chickens
  Life's swell down on the farm.

Sixty Minutes

"Sixty minutes!" Mom defies---
While coffee perks she makes two pies,
She tosses laundry in machine
And grabs the sweeper, floors to clean.
She calmly lists all she can do
And wisely makes a follow-through.
Her hour is full. She doesn't mind…
She leaves a trail of work behind.

Now dad awakes and spies the clock---
An hour early…what a shock!
He blinks and rubs his tired eyes,
Decides more sleeping would be wise;
So calmly, too, he takes a stand,
Goes back to bed and sweet dreamland.
Those extra moments mean more rest,
And this he needs to work his best.

"A whole long hour," says little sis,
"Before to school…I can't stand this!"
She nibbles breakfast, oh so slow,
And wonders "Will it ever snow?"
Then quietly she finds a book
And settles self in a cozy nook,
Awaiting hands of time's slow turning,
The endless space of childhood's yearning.

For teenage princess---it's a price,
She jumps and yells, "An hour! My gosh!"
"I simply must call Linda, quick---
She doesn't know I talked to Rick.
Betty wants a reference page,
And Julie asked for that hem gauge.
Judy didn't call last night.
I've got to see if she's alright!"

"Good grief, my hair is such a mess---
And oh yes, where's my Home-Ec dress?
Did either of you see my ring?
And what did Edith say to bring?
Where is my other pair of shoes?
And get the money for class dues!
Who put my lipstick in the bed?
And where's a scarf for on my head?"

"Who moved my notebook on the floor?
Oh, I forgot that football score!
My crewneck's gone---I need it, too,
No, not the brown one, that dark blue.
I want a sack for P.T. clothes,
And find a pair of seamless hose.
Please hurry Mom, you just don't know
How fast that Sixty Minutes goes!"

Slippin'

Said the slippery bark
To the old elm tree,
"You can't hang on
Anymore to me---
      I'm slippin."

Said the baby beaver
As he went down the slide,
"Catch me mama,
I've ruined my hide---
      I'm slippin."

Said the old gray goose
On the cold lake ice,
"I can't swim in this,
It's cold, by gosh---
      I'm slippin."

Said Ma to Pa
With a gasp and sigh,
"Forgot my friend's birthday,
I could almost cry---
      I'm slippin."

There isn't any moral,
This story's gettin' old,
---But so am I---
My tale is told---
      I'm slippin.

Summer Sickness

Howdy, fellars, Howdy! Can you guess what brings me here?

I'm the sickest, sickest youngin!…for me yer gonna fear.

See how pale and puny I'm a lookin' these here days,

Grandma thinks its measles…"A youngin' takes 'em this here way."

Mama says, "Oh 'tisn't nothin', just a cold or somethun' like."

But daddy says, "My little girl's a lookin' mighty white."

Grandad says, "It's weather makes a kid grow kinda thin."

But I got 'em fooled, I betcha, even includin' him.

'Cause I get a sickish feelin'

Whether weather's hot or cool,

When I think that come September

I've got to go to school!

> *Written for our 5 year old daughter in 1953*
> *to speak at the School Alumni Picnic*
> *for which she received $2.50 for third place.*

Alphabetical Listing

About the Author

Raised in the countryside of Northern Missouri, Dorothy had many rich opportunities to glean material for her future compositions. These life experiences enabled her to write of many varied topics including her deep faith, fascinations impacting her, festivities in her life, the folks surrounding, and inevitably the fun which exemplifies the humor threaded throughout Dorothy's life.

As a child, she often sang at the piano with her mother playing at the keys. These rhythms continued for her onto paper over the expanse of more than 35 years, although free verse form and prose are also talents her readers enjoy. Much of her work is memory related, and indeed to those of us privileged to know her, touches us with love.

Printed in the United States
34672LVS00005B/1-60

9 781420 860009